MW00782623

Nods of approval for *Growing With Eli*

Growing with Eli – the third book in the trilogy about Eli's early years – will lift your hearts and minds to see the presence of the Lord in the ordinary and extra-ordinary moments of life. It will help you to recognize each and every person's life – at all times and in all circumstances – as a gift from God.

I highly recommend *Growing with Eli* and Chad Judice's previous books to all who would benefit from accessible and moving accounts of the goodness of the Lord present in our lives.

Cardinal Seán O'Malley, OFM, Cap.
Archbishop of Boston

*   *   *

What a powerful book! Every man needs to read this to be a better father, friend and husband! Chad will share with you, through the example of his life, how men can learn to pray and become men who live a life of courage and trust in God in spite of any circumstance.

Fr. Larry Richards
Founder, The Reason for Our Hope Foundation
EWTN syndicated radio personality

*   *   *

This book opens up a great truth: At times, God uses suffering and difficulty to get our heart's attention.

The book is a journey that recognizes that living out the Catholic faith is not, as many suggest, just about obeying a set of rules. Behind the "rules" is a person; faith is about being in love with Jesus Christ.

It is a page-turner that brings to life the necessity of good, holy friendships; facing with honesty the struggles of marriage; and illustrating that lives are ultimately defined by the decision to love.

Fr. Michael Russo, Pastor
Our Lady of Fatima Catholic Church
Lafayette, Louisiana

GROWING WITH
ELI

Our Journey into Life and Light

Chad Judice

Acadian House
PUBLISHING
Lafayette, Louisiana

The Acadian House Publishing Speakers Bureau can bring authors
to your live event. For more information or to book an author, contact
Acadian House Publishing at (337) 235-8851, Ext. 104, or
info@acadianhouse.com.

Library of Congress Cataloging-in-Publication Data

Names: Judice, Chad.
Title: Growing with Eli : our journey into life and light / Chad Judice.
Description: Lafayette, LA : Acadian House Publishing, 2018. | Includes
    bibliographical references and index.
Identifiers: LCCN 2018014138 | ISBN 9780999588420 (hardcover) |
    ISBN 0999588427 (hardcover)
Subjects: LCSH: Judice, Eli, 2009---Health. | Spina bifida--
    Patients--Louisiana--Lafayette--Biography. | Spina bifida--
    Patients--Family relationships. | Fathers--Religious life.
Classification: LCC RJ496.S74 J84 2018 | DDC 617.4/82092 [B] --dc23
LC record available at https://lccn.loc.gov/2018014138

♦ Published by Acadian House Publishing, Lafayette, Louisiana
  (Edited by Trent Angers; editorial assistance and research by Darlene Smith;
  design and pre-press production by Leah Ewing)
♦ Printed by Sheridan Books, Chelsea, Michigan

For Ashley

Preface

The third book of a pro-life trilogy

Eli Judice was destined to be well known. He was the subject of a book even before he was one year old.

Now that he's nine, he's the subject of three books.

This book is the third of a trilogy featuring this special-needs child and his family, told from the perspective of the boy's father.

The first was *Waiting For Eli: A Father's Journey from Fear to Faith*; then came *Eli's Reach: On the Value of Human Life and the Power of Prayer*; and now *Growing With Eli: Our Journey into Life and Light*.

Book 1 describes the family's anxious wait for Eli's birth and his coming into the world with a dreaded defect called *spina bifida*. Book 2 deals with the impact Eli's story has had on others, drawing some into more fervent prayer and inspiring some to reject abortion and choose life for their unborn babies.

Book 3 tracks Eli's growth from his earliest years into a healthy, happy second-grader. And at the same time, on a parallel track, this volume chronicles the growth of Eli's father, Chad Judice, in his understanding and practice of his Catholic faith.

Eli makes his grand entrance into the world on February 17, 2009, in a hospital in Metairie, La., and undergoes the first of several surgeries only days after his birth. We see him a year or so later at home "army-crawling" on his elbows and dragging his paralyzed legs behind him. A few years later, he's rolling into kindergarten in his wheelchair, and horsing around with his big brother, Ephraim, at the beach in Alabama. We see him being introduced to adoring fans following his dad's presentations around Louisiana – and even once in Washington, D.C., during the big annual March for Life events.

One of the notable sub-plots of the new book deals with Chad's internal conflict on whether to stick with and truly embrace his chosen profession of teaching or to change careers into that of a fulltime writer and public speaker. In his heart of hearts, he wants to travel the country telling Eli's story, for this is one of the main things he believes he was put on this earth to do. But then comes the sobering question of how to support a family without a steady, guaranteed paycheck.

Chad and Eli don't walk alone on their journey, of course. The Lord is with them, and they have a dependable earthly support system. They're part of a family that includes Ashley, Chad's wife and Eli's mom; Ephraim, Eli's big brother; and Chad's parents and Ashley's parents, who help – a lot – to care for the children. Then there are members of Chad's men's prayer group who help one another to grow in their pursuit of Christian manhood – as iron sharpens iron. Plus Chad wisely avails himself of spiritual advisors, two priests who at various times are there for him in his hours of need.

The book also tells of Chad and Ashley's devotion to the Blessed Virgin Mary and their rejection of artificial contraception in their pursuit of a truly sacramental marriage.

Growing With Eli is a frank and very personal account of the lives of a special-needs boy and his dad, both of whom valiantly fight their way through all that life can throw at them. But, in the final analysis, this is simply a pro-life story. The critical juncture occurs soon after Chad and Ashley learn of Eli's diagnosis – *spina bifida* – and make the decision to go forward with the pregnancy. They respond with a resounding "yes" to God's will and to the life of their unborn son. And what a beautiful life it proves to be.

– *Trent Angers, OFS*
Editor & Publisher

Foreword

On manning-up

I first met Chad Judice when he was a teacher and coach at Cathedral Carmel School in Lafayette, Louisiana. It was clear to me that he was a young man of great passion and intensity. At the time, he had no idea that God had a plan to use these gifts to inspire so many to learn the power of prayer and faith, courage and fortitude.

God's plan would be realized in the birth of a truly beautiful child with special needs – the one thing that Chad feared more than anything. Salvation history has shown that the Lord has a way of using things a man fears the most to bring him to the place He wants him to be. Thus, the birth of Elijah Paul Judice would mark a new beginning in the life of Chad Judice, his wife Ashley, and their first son, Ephraim.

What has unfolded since then is nothing short of a miracle, given the vitality and growth of young Eli and the faith, courage and resolve of his father and family to persevere in prayer and hope. It is the miracle of what grace can do for a person who must quickly and decisively move from fear to faith, from despair to hope, from self-love to sacrificial love. The story shared in the following pages is of one man's journey to embrace this crusade.

There is no doubt that in the world of today, the Church of today, there is a need for that crusade to be taken up in every place and culture. Study after study shows the devastating effects of the failure of so many to be men after God's own heart. How many children today suffer from the heartbreak of growing up without the presence – be it physical, spiritual or moral – of a strong father? This absence is seen all too clearly in churches everywhere in which we find mothers with children and no father by their side to teach their children that faith, hope, love and right worship are essential to real manliness. Far too many men have left women and children to fend for themselves due to a lack of maturity and a wealth of selfishness.

In this stirring work of literary humility, a young husband and new father reveals an understanding of what it means to man-up while striving to become a man after God's own heart. The road to real manhood is marked by trial and sacrifice, intense prayer and at times copious tears. Still, it's a road a man must travel if he wishes to become all that God has created him to be.

In this book you will meet, or be reunited with, one man who made the decision not to run and hide but to stand and fight the good fight of faith – and to sacrifice himself for those he was called to protect.

– *Fr. Matthew P. Higginbotham,* Pastor
  Immaculate Conception Catholic Church
  Washington, Louisiana

Contents

Preface...6

Foreword..9

1. Eli is growing up, and so am I.....................15

2. So, God really loves us?.............................23

3. Iron sharpens iron....................................31

4. The death of illusion.................................37

5. Eli comes into the world............................43

6. What more do you want, Lord?..................47

7. Opening our minds
   to Natural Family Planning.......................55

8. Who's the impaired one here, anyway?...................61

9. Eli's big brother: a kind, gentle soul.......................75

10. Whispers of a third child.....................................79

11. Our Lady of Mt. Carmel, pray for us!....................87

12. A companion on the journey...............................95

13. Dark night of the soul.......................................101

14. A divine appointment on Highway 90..................113

15. Miriam's Song...117

16. The circle of life...123

Afterword: *Waiting For Eli* – The movie?............................131

Appendix...133

Sources..141

References..144

Index...147

About the Author..157

GROWING WITH
ELI

Chapter 1

Eli is growing up, and so am I

Writers who are passionate about the story they want to tell have a few things in common. First and foremost, we want to tell the world.

Texting it to friends and family isn't enough. Posting it on Facebook reaches too limited of an audience. Writing a letter to the editor usually gets to only a modest number of people.

My story basically is about my son, Eli, who was born with a dreaded birth defect called *spina bifida*. It's also about how his birth has transformed my life and that of my family – and touched the hearts and minds of many thousands of people throughout the United States.

Now, I did have opportunities to tell the world, more or less, when I was a guest on the global Catholic

network, EWTN (Eternal Word Television Network).
I appeared twice, once in May of 2013 on "The World
Over" with Raymond Arroyo, and again in November
of 2015 on a program called "At Home with Jim and
Joy Pinto."

Besides that, the *New York Post* ran an abbreviated
version of Eli's story, as an op-ed piece, which reached
several hundred thousand readers in the New York
metropolitan area. Here's what they published in
August of 2014:

How choosing life
changed everything

*Last week I dropped off my son Eli for his first day
of kindergarten – got him out of the car and into his
wheelchair and rolled him into the classroom.*

*It was the proudest day of my life, and of course
brought to mind the hardest days – the one when the
doctor told us our unborn son had the birth defect
spina bifida, and the one when we got the follow-up
question: "Would you like to terminate the pregnancy?"*

*With a college degree, a good job as a teacher
and coach, a beautiful wife (really, she's gorgeous), a
healthy son and another child on the way, my hopes for
the future were boundless that day in the fall of 2008.*

*I was also under the illusion that I was very much
in control of my life – a control freak, type-A to the
max. That illusion of control was shattered – big time
– when we got the diagnosis.*

I spent the rest of that day dazed and terrified. How would this affect our marriage? Our older son? Our finances?

The next day, the doctor asked about abortion. My wife Ashley replied with an adamant no. Both of us believe in the value of every human life from the moment of conception.

That evening, though, Ashley cried as she read to me from the literature we'd been given. It said 80 percent of parents who receive a spina bifida diagnosis choose abortion.

And it told us that our son might have learning disabilities and be paralyzed from the waist down, unable to ever walk.

Ashley is a nurse who cares for sick newborns and premature babies in our hospital's NICU, but this news left her cold with fear at the suffering our child would face.

But still, in a spirit of trust in God, we chose to reject abortion and welcome Elijah Paul into our lives.

And, yes, we prayed for a miracle. We were joined in prayer by our relatives, friends, my students at a Lafayette, La., Catholic school and even by complete strangers.

Heck, getting high-school students to a place of heartfelt prayer was something of a miracle by itself, but such was the compelling nature of Eli's story even then.

Eli was born on Feb. 17, 2009. He did have spina

bifida, but the opening in his spine, which doctors had warned us might be as big as a softball, was just a little bigger than the size of a quarter. His surgeries went well, and despite the medical challenges, he was home in less than a month.

Living with Eli has been an adventure.... And as we continue our journey, Ashley and I have been through experiences that have scared the daylights out of us.

But our boy is doing well – better than the doctors ever expected. With braces and a special device, he's learning to walk. His intelligence is at or above average, and he's very talkative.

Most important, he's a happy child with a beautiful smile and a twinkle in his eye.

I think of Eli as God's special gift to my family. And as I share about him, Eli's story softens hearts and brings people to a greater appreciation of the beauty and sacredness of life.

Hearing it, some pregnant mothers – four or five that I know of – have been moved to reject abortion. Several times, I've also seen Eli's story rekindle the dormant faith of some – including men – drawing them into a life with more room for God and family.

One guy who had basically given up on God after many years in prison read my first book and was moved to tears, literally. Eli's story broke that heart of stone, and the man prayed for Eli's health and well-being as he recited The Lord's Prayer. It was the first *time he'd prayed in 30 years.*

My first book, by the way, is titled Waiting for Eli: A Father's Journey from Fear to Faith, *and my second is* Eli's Reach: On the Value of Human Life and the Power of Prayer.

I've traveled the country telling Eli's story – that rather than abort our baby, as 80 percent of Americans would have, we chose life for him and brought a happy, beautiful baby into the world.

Bringing Eli to term – giving him a chance at life – was the right thing to do. I'm reminded of it every evening, when I kiss and say good night to my beautiful boy.

In addition to writing for newspapers and online newsletters and speaking on radio and television, I made more than a hundred presentations in person in 17 states over a seven-year span. I've spoken in Texas, Louisiana and Florida, as well as New York, New Jersey and Washington, D.C., and elsewhere. (As you can see, I've been trying to tell the world about my son and the impact his life has had on others around the country.)

Audiences seem to be moved by the story. They're quiet and very polite; some even seem to be downright enthralled. Many of the women cry; some of the men do as well. They respond to the pro-life message of Eli's story; their hearts go out to the little boy in the wheelchair whose parents welcomed him into the

HOW CHOOSING LIFE CHANGED EVERYTHING

LAST week, I dropped off my son Eli for his first day of kindergarten — got him out of the car and into his wheelchair and rolled him into the classroom.

It was the proudest day of my life, and of course brought to mind the hardest days — the one when the doctor told us our unborn son had the birth defect spine bifida, and the one when we got the follow-up question: "Would you like to terminate the pregnancy?"

With a college degree, a good job as a teacher and coach, a beautiful wife (really, she's gorgeous), a healthy son and another child on the way, my hopes for the future were boundless that day in the fall of 2008.

I was also under the illusion that I was very much in control of my life — a control freak, type-A to the max. That illusion was shattered — big time — when we got the diagnosis.

I spent the rest of that day dazed and terrified. How would this affect our marriage? Our older son? Our finances?

The next day, the doctor asked about abortion. My wife Ashley replied with an adamant no. Both of us believe in the value of every human life from the moment of conception.

That evening, though, Ashley cried as she read to me from the literature we'd been given. It said 90 percent of parents who receive a spina bifida diagnosis choose abortion.

And, it told us that our son might have learning disabilities and be paralyzed from the waist down, unable to ever walk.

Ashley is a nurse who cares for newborns in our hospital's ICU, but this news left her cold with fear at the suffering our child would face.

But still, in a spirit of trust in God, we chose to reject abortion and welcome Elijah Paul into our lives.

And, yes, we prayed for a mir-

CHAD JUDICE

average, and he's very talkative.

Most important, he's a happy child with a beautiful smile and a twinkle in his eye.

I think of Eli as God's special gift to my family. And as I share about him, Eli's story softens hearts and brings people to a greater appreciation of the beauty and sacredness of life.

Hearing it, some pregnant mothers — four or five that I know of — have been moved to reject abortion. Several times, I've also seen Eli's story rekindle the dormant faith of some

> ❝ He's a happy child with a beautiful smile and a twinkle in his eye. ❞

acle. We were joined in prayer by our relatives, friends, my students at a Lafayette, La., Catholic school and even by complete strangers.

Heck, getting high-school students to a place of heartfelt prayer was something of a miracle by itself, but such was the compelling nature of Eli's story even then.

Eli was born on Feb. 17, 2009. He did have spina bifida, but the opening in his spine, which doctors had warned us might be as big as a softball, was just the size of a quarter. His surgeries went well, and despite the medical challenges, he was home in less than a month.

Living with Eli has been an adventure. He's had seizures and surgeries, and as we continue our journey, Ashley and I have been through experiences that have scared the daylights out of us.

But our boy is doing well — better than the doctors ever expected. With braces and a special device, he's learning to walk. His intelligence is at or above

— including men — drawing them into a life with more room for God and family.

One guy who had basically given up on God after many years in prison read my first book and was moved to tears. Literally, Eli's story broke the heart of stone, and the man prayed for Eli's health and well-being as he recited The Lord's Prayer. It was the first time he'd prayed in 30 years.

I've traveled the country telling Eli's story — that rather than abort our baby, as 90 percent of Americans would have, we chose life for him and brought a happy, beautiful baby into the world.

Bringing Eli to term — giving him a chance at life — was the right thing to do. I'm reminded of it every evening, when I kiss and say good night to my beautiful boy.

Chad Judice (chadjudice.com) is the author of "Waiting for Eli: A Father's Journey from Fear to Faith" and "Eli's Reach: On the Value of Human Life and the Power of Prayer."

world rather than choosing to end his life while in the womb.

I've come to believe that telling Eli's story is what I was put on this earth to do – that, and being a family man and a teacher of theology.

As Eli continues to grow up, so do I. Our stories are intertwined; our lives move forward together. Eli has come through multiple surgeries, several seizures and countless physical therapy sessions. He has attended Pre-K, kindergarten and first grade and has moved into second grade. At the same time, my faith in God has grown by leaps and bounds as I have plumbed the depth and breadth of the Catholic religion. I've discovered, to my amazement, tenets of the faith I didn't understand so well in the past. These include the life-altering power of forgiveness, the meaning of a truly sacramental marriage, the Church's teachings on Natural Family Planning, and the role of the Blessed Virgin Mary as the great intercessor.

But life hasn't been easy – for me, for Eli, nor for the rest of our family.

Chapter 2

So, God really loves us?

A pivotal chapter in our story as a family began on a warm, clear Friday afternoon in May of 2004. Eli wasn't even a twinkle in my eye at the time, and his older brother, Ephraim, hadn't been born yet either.

I pulled into my driveway, looking forward to seeing my wife Ashley's smiling face. I was 27 years old and felt like I was on top of the world.

I had just wrapped up another workday at Cathedral-Carmel, a small Catholic school in our hometown of Lafayette, La., where I coached basketball and taught social studies to seventh and eighth graders.

I got out of my car, walked into our house, and found Ashley sitting in her favorite chair in the living room, with a whimsical look in her eye. I leaned in for a kiss. Then she stood and handed me a small cell phone that looked like a toy.

I examined it briefly, then blurted out with a hint of sarcasm:

"What's this for? It's a toy. Something for a baby?"

Ashley smiled, then I heard the words that should have filled my heart with joy and excitement.

"I'm pregnant," she said with a smile that lit up the room.

I thought I was ready to hear those words, but when they came out my heart fell into my stomach. Fear and anxiety shot through my gut. Time seemed to stop. For the next few minutes I tried to get my mind around what this meant. I was going to be a dad. Wow! I was now responsible for another human being and would be for the next 21 years or so.

I sat there crying. I presume Ashley thought it was a combination of excitement and shock, but truthfully I was overwhelmed at the thought of it.

And that's when I began to run – psychologically and spiritually.

We had been together for six years, had careers with a good degree of financial stability, and had already ridden the roller coaster ride of a young married couple for the previous four years. Yes, we had made a lifelong commitment to one another before God, but for the first time ever it felt really, really permanent.

With this journey as parents beginning to unfold, instead of drawing closer to Ashley and our unborn child, I felt like a scared little boy who was being forced to face the reality of fatherhood. I believed in my heart that I was embracing this new responsibility, but my behavior indicated otherwise. For the first time in our marriage, I began to focus on things about Ashley that I hadn't been outwardly critical of in the past – things I had disregarded while we were dating and in the earliest years of our marriage.

Our arguments were typical of married couples preparing for their first child: money and finances, differing philosophies on parenting, how we envisioned the changes that were to come in our lives after the birth of our child. Despite this normal tension, I marveled at the way Ashley embraced the call of motherhood while actively bonding with this new life she was carrying.

Outwardly, I thought I was doing everything right and maintaining a happy disposition, but I didn't have the strong personal connection to the concept of parenthood the way Ashley did.

Inwardly, I was in crisis – and on the verge of completely losing all physical attraction to my wife, even though she is one of the most beautiful women I have ever seen.

As the weeks and months dragged on, romantic moments were few and far between. In place of intimacy, I began to look closely at the attractive women at the health club to which I belonged. I talked often with a few of them; their attention and compliments

Area of Louisiana where Eli's story unfolds

seemed to meet one of my subconscious desires. I confess, carrying on in this manner was a form of unfaithfulness, though it never crossed the line to physical infidelity.

*   *   *

Ephraim's birth changed me. It changed my perception of God the Father. Before Ephraim was born, my understanding of God had been that He was something, not someone. I had always heard "God loves you," but the meaning of this message never sank in completely. Maybe I never felt worthy of His love; I'm not sure.

But something happened to me when I held Ephraim for the first time, something wonderful and profound. I became super-vigilant, totally alive, deeply committed to providing for him and his mother – and nothing was going to stop me. My love for this baby was strong; I loved him unconditionally, absolutely, deeply. And if I loved him this much, was it possible that God the Father – our Father – could love us even more than that? Infinitely more? How could that be possible?

The very thought of this brought tears of joy to my eyes; the contemplation of it left me wonderstruck. I kept repeating, *Oh, my God! Oh, my God, Abba, Father...*

I basked in the thought of it: God really does love us in a way and to a depth that's beyond our ability to comprehend.

*   *   *

Unfortunately, my epiphany, as beautiful as it was, was short-lived. A month or two after the birth of our son, it was clear to me that things had changed in our marriage – and it seemed they would never be the way they were before. Once we returned home from the hospital, Ashley's entire focus was on Ephraim. Our marital bond was not strong at the time, and trying to re-establish it without God at the center of our lives wasn't working out so well.

Like many women who have just had a baby, Ashley had hormonal issues that clearly impacted her personality – and not in a way that I thought of as positive. My desire for things to be the way they were before the pregnancy only increased as our affection for one another seemed to decrease. As Ashley struggled to lose weight, I held an image in my mind of what I thought she should be, instead of recognizing her for the beautiful person that she was. My will was weak, my thoughts were dark and negative, and my appreciation for Ashley was at a low ebb.

But despite my ingratitude, the Lord blessed us with some great news three months after the birth of our child. I was called back to St. Thomas More High School for a second interview for a job as a member of the faculty. I'd applied prior to the current school year, but the job had gone to another applicant. This time, I got the job.

STM is where I wanted to be, and I thought that being there would make me happy. But I would soon figure out that there's more to happiness than having the right job.

Chapter 3

Iron sharpens iron

S oon after starting the job at STM, I was invited to join a men's prayer group made up of married male teachers. We met monthly over supper at the home of Fr. Joe Breaux, our school's chaplain and pastor of a church in a nearby community.

The purpose of these gatherings was to learn more about our Savior and about ourselves. It was an exercise in self-discovery designed to deepen our understanding of Jesus Christ and to cultivate a *bona fide* friendship with Him. Another of our goals was to define, or re-define, the meaning of manhood – a definition that would run counter to the impressions held by secular society in our country.

My perception of real manhood had been seriously distorted by the culture in which I grew up. Prior to our numerous group discussions, I understood manhood to mean physical strength, sound-mindedness, financial success, and achievement in my career.

I, for one, didn't understand that vulnerability and sensitivity are indicators of strength, not weakness. Growing up, my friendships had nothing to do with Christian values, but rather were tied to worldly pursuits. Things like piety, contemplation and reverence were reserved for the one hour during which I attended Mass, my "Sunday obligation." The concept of connecting the life and teachings of Jesus Christ to my everyday life was foreign to me.

The other three men in our group seemed to be further along in their spiritual maturity than I. They seemed more self-confident. They appeared to be truly selfless people. I couldn't say the same for myself.

I wanted what they had.

In the course of dialogue at these suppers, it became clear to me that, for most of my life, I had carried a certain emptiness inside. I longed for something to fill this void, this sense of being incomplete. I wanted to become the man I was created to be, but I wasn't sure how to get there.

As we opened up to one another over supper, I came to realize that the only thing big enough to fill that emptiness in me was God Himself.

Among the key reasons for our meetings was to help us to live in accordance with our school's mission statement: We were to educate our students to become "seekers of truth, individuals of character, and God's servant first." The men in our group were committed to modeling this behavior for the entire student body, starting with the seniors, in hopes that they would follow our example.

One of the recurring themes of our gatherings was the concept of dying to oneself for the benefit of others, especially for our loved ones. We were meant to become "men for others," as the Jesuits like to say, and not self-serving seekers of wealth, power and prestige.

Through dialogue, we recognized that our talents, our good health and material assets were gifts from God. We were merely stewards of these gifts. With this in mind, we came to appreciate the meaning of a prayer written by St. Ignatius, founder of the Society of Jesus, the Jesuits.

> *Take and receive, O Lord, all my liberty, my memory, my understanding and my entire will. All that I have and possess You have given to me. To You, O Lord, I return them. They are Yours; do with them what You will. Give me Your love and Your grace, for this is sufficient for me; and I am rich enough and ask for nothing more. Amen.*

Our group discussions were usually guided by the Gospel message to be read at the upcoming Sunday Mass. Fr. Joe would read the Gospel then pose a question or two about our lives, which we were to answer in a spiritual context.

Everyone seemed to speak frankly and openly. Their honesty impressed me. I had never heard men speak with such certainty, such faith about God.

In traveling this journey towards Christian manhood, we were always aware that we were helping each other to grow in knowledge, strength and resolve. We shared our innermost thoughts and feelings, sometimes challenging each other's thinking – though in a constructive way. We were all keenly aware of a certain Scriptural passage that could have been our mantra:

> *People learn from one another,*
> *just as iron sharpens iron.*
> (Proverbs 27:17)

*   *   *

During my second year at STM, I was asked to give a talk at our annual faculty retreat. The theme was "Respect," and the audience came to about 100 teachers. Though I had been prepared in spirit by the meaningful discussions of our prayer group, I was nervous and uncomfortable and feeling a bit unworthy to be speaking before such a crowd. But despite my insecurities, the presentation seemed to be well-received.

Thus, I had taken my first steps down a path I never thought I would travel: speaking publicly about my beliefs, my values and my personal experiences. As it would turn out, this is a path I was destined to travel – speaking with passion and deep conviction about a special-needs child who would be coming into the world in the not-too-distant future.

Chapter 4

The death of illusion

In June of 2008, Ashley announced that we were expecting our second child. We were excited as parents and pleased about the idea that Ephraim would soon have a brother or sister.

A couple months later, Ephraim, age three at the time, and I were at Mass while Ashley was at work. She worked as a neonatal intensive care nurse at a hospital in Lafayette.

Dear God, please let our new baby be born healthy. That's all I ask, I prayed in silence, staring at the crucifix behind the altar while holding Ephraim on my lap.

At the same time, my greatest fear in the world – as I had stated out loud on several occasions in the past – was to have a child born with a mental or physical handicap. I didn't think I was strong enough to handle such a responsibility; I lacked the parenting skills, especially the patience.

Sixteen weeks into the pregnancy, Ashley and I went to the doctor's office for a routine ultrasound. Through this common imaging procedure, we would hear the baby's heartbeat, see the internal organs, and learn whether we had a boy or a girl. We hoped to learn firsthand that everything was okay and that the baby was healthy.

But everything was not okay. Something was missing. The technician couldn't locate part of the baby's brain.

Thus, in that moment, my greatest fear became my reality.

It was the shock of our lives. We cried. I got weak in the knees and had to sit down. *This can't be. There must be some mistake. This can't be happening to us and our baby.*

But there was no mistake. The reading was accurate. Our unborn child was displaying one of the classic, unmistakable signs of *spina bifida*.

Now, for all of our lives, Ashley and I had honored God, though we never thought of ourselves as desperate for Him. But that changed that fateful day as we realized how small we were and how dependent upon God we truly were.

For most of my life up until that point, I had been living with the idea that I was in control of my life. I was "master of my fate, captain of my soul," as the poet William Ernest Henley says in *Invictus.*

But that illusion died a sudden death that day in the darkness of the ultrasound room, on September 30, 2008.

That same night, still in shock and disbelief, Ashley and I read up on *spina bifida* and what effects it could have on our child's quality of life. What we learned was depressing: paralysis from the waist on down, possible learning disabilities, absence of control of the bowels, and the need to be catheterized multiple times per day to prevent kidney infections and other health problems. And the list went on. The literature also noted that 80 percent of Americans presented with this prenatal diagnosis choose to abort their unborn babies.

We talked about that option for less than a minute, then dismissed it out of hand. It was only a passing thought – never seriously considered. This was a human being, for God's sake, our own flesh and blood! He was our baby, a special child sent to us by the Creator of life. We would bring our baby to term, trust in God's providence and pray for His mercy.

We decided to give our child a biblical name, as we had done for his brother, Ephraim. We would call him Elijah Paul Judice, "Eli" for short.

*   *   *

The *spina bifida* diagnosis brought me to my knees,

literally. And while on my knees, I began to pray more sincerely, more fervently than I ever had. That day, in September of 2008, I began a new life.

I turned to Mary, the mother of Jesus, in prayer. Who better to understand the awful, helpless feeling of knowing one's child is suffering while being unable to do anything about it? As a child relies on his mother for protection and comfort, I begged Mother Mary for help – praying that she intercede with her son, Jesus, in asking for a miracle to cure my son, Eli.

Soon I was praying the Rosary daily – the Hail Marys, Our Fathers and Glory Be's. With each decade, I meditated on the mysteries of the Rosary, recounting the various episodes in the life of Christ. The Joyful Mysteries include the birth of Jesus and His mission to redeem humankind from sin. The Sorrowful Mysteries – with which I identified most closely at the time – include the Lord's agony in the garden, His carrying of the cross, and His crucifixion and death. Among the Glorious Mysteries are Jesus' resurrection from the dead and His ascension into Heaven. The Luminous Mysteries cover Jesus' baptism in the River Jordan, His proclamation that the Kingdom of God is at hand, and other events described in the Gospels. (See Appendix for a complete list of the mysteries and brief descriptions of each.)

I prayed the Rosary every day, sometimes more than once. This practice didn't wane after a week or a month or a few months, but would become and remain the staple of my prayer life.

Mother Mary accompanied Ashley and me on our journey while waiting for Eli to be born. She would continue to be a mother to us in our times of confusion and uncertainty, helping us to find shelter from the storm as we prayed the Rosary and grew in our trust of the Lord.

Chapter 5

Eli comes into the world

E li was born by way of Cesarean section on February 17, 2009, at Tulane-Lakeside Hospital in Metairie, La., a city adjacent to New Orleans. I was allowed to hold him for a very short while, maybe a minute or two, before he was taken from the birthing room.

A couple days later, Eli underwent two surgeries simultaneously – one to sew up a lesion in his back (common in babies born with *spina bifida*) and the other to insert a shunt in his head to control the flow of spinal fluid up and down the spinal cord to the ventricles of the brain. (Hydrocephalus, or "water on the brain," is common in infants with *spina bifida*; insertion of the shunt is standard operating procedure.)

Seeing Eli in recovery in the Neonatal Intensive

Care Unit following surgery was heartrending. He was so small, totally helpless, hooked up to all sorts of wires and tubes, and surely in some degree of pain.

The jumble of emotions running through me included gratitude, too: I thanked God Eli was receiving the best medical care the world had to offer. How fortunate we were in this regard.

After being in the hospital a few days for Eli's birth and surgeries, it was time for me to return to Lafayette to go back to work and to resume caring for Ephraim. My parents had been with him while we were out of town. Ashley and Eli would stay in the hospital a while longer. Ashley's parents, who had joined us at the hospital, would remain nearby so they could continue helping in any way possible.

Following the resolution of a few medical complications, Ashley and Eli were discharged about two weeks after I left.

Soon after returning to Lafayette, I began telling Eli's story to practically anyone or any group who would listen. Each time, I asked for the audience's prayers for Eli and for our family. I spoke to a local Confirmation class a week after my return, then to a gathering of the Secular Franciscans (the Third Order of St. Francis), then to various pro-life groups, as well as high school and college students in Louisiana and Texas. I even got to address the entire St. Thomas More community – students, faculty, staff and parents.

The year following Eli's birth was tiring for me and challenging in my role as father, husband, teacher and now frequent public speaker. Ashley and I continued to pray the Rosary every day, I in the chapel at STM and she at home while caring for our children. Sometimes we prayed it together.

*　　*　　*

When Eli was about a year old, he started to crawl on his elbows while dragging his legs behind him. We called it "army-crawling."

Eli's condition required infant physical therapy and occupational therapy at home. We were visited by a physical therapist weekly and by an occupational therapist on alternating weeks. Ashley and I reinforced what they were doing, helping Eli with the exercises on the days they weren't there.

We loved this little boy so much, and we felt fiercely protective of him. There was nothing in the world we wouldn't do to help him enjoy the best possible quality of life.

Chapter 6

What more do You want, Lord?

I f you want to give God a good laugh, tell Him what your plans are!

I've heard this witty saying for many years, and I believe there's a lot of truth in it. Ashley and I even have a little magnet sign on our refrigerator that says "We plan, God laughs!"

I have been a planner all my life, and I've learned first-hand that it's God's plans, not mine, that come to pass.

My plan was to teach history and coach basketball until retirement. Then Eli was born, and everything changed. Today, I no longer teach history or coach at all. Instead, I'm engaged in three pursuits I never envisioned: writing, public speaking and teaching Catholic high school students subjects such as social justice,

Church history, and the Theology of the Body.

The stress, uncertainty and sense of urgency Ashley and I have experienced with Eli's condition has had a huge impact on our lives and on our marriage. Early on, one thing that stressed us to the max was the need to cathetherize Eli five times a day. This was necessary in order to prevent kidney infections and other serious health problems. One of the effects of *spina bifida* is that the bladder doesn't drain completely on its own, and the catheter helps it to do so, thus reducing the risk of infection in that area.

The entire experience of having a special-needs child, while it seemed to challenge the very existence of our marriage, has ultimately strengthened our relationship. Still, given the fact that the divorce rate for couples in situations like ours is as high as 80 percent, I knew a conscious effort was needed by both Ashley and me to re-enliven and solidify our marriage. This is what I prayed for much of the time during my daily visits to the chapel at St. Thomas More.

The answer I was searching for came in the most unexpected way.

As I prayed for help and guidance, I became aware of a stronger and stronger desire to grow in knowledge of the Catholic faith. This hunger was not something I could account for on my own; I consider it a gift from above. I was devouring Scripture every chance I could and discovering that the more I grew in love for the Lord, the more I grew in love for the Church.

However, there was one area I was finding reasons to avoid learning more about: the Church's teachings on the use of artificial contraception.

A 2013 Gallup poll indicates that more than 82 percent of Amercan Roman Catholics say contraception is morally acceptable. Only 15 percent say it is not acceptable, while 3 percent say it depends on specific circumstances.

Though I knew there was a deeper explanation to the Church's teaching, I continued to justify the use of artificial contraception due to our circumstances. Genetic testing following Eli's birth had led Ashley and me to believe there was a higher chance of the same birth defect occurring in the next child we might conceive.

At the time, I felt we had more than enough challenges and uncertainties to deal with. I was willing to accept self-imposed ignorance on the issue of artificial contraception; I was applying my own moral standard. I might have been sharing a powerful message in public about surrender and total trust in God, but this was one thing I was not willing to give up.

I knew that if the Church could provide as convincing an answer on this difficult issue as it had on everything else, I would have to change my behavior. Instinctively, I resorted to a familiar habit to deal with Church teachings I was not comfortable with: bargaining with God.

*   *   *

I realized that God wanted all my love, all my devotion, without reservation. And He wanted my full adherence to the teachings of the Church.

This belief was reinforced in me by meditation on the Gospel story in which Jesus is asked by a rich man what more he must do to receive eternal life. The man hastens to point out that since his youth he has faithfully obeyed the Ten Commandments. The Scripture continues:

> *Jesus looked straight at him with love and said, "You need only one thing. Go and sell all you have and give the money to the poor, and you will have riches in heaven; then come and follow me."*
>
> *When the man heard this, gloom spread over his face, and he went away sad, because he was very rich.* (Mark 10:21-22)

I related so well to that rich man. I have had pretty much the same conversation with Jesus on the subject of not holding back. I was holding on to something He wanted me to surrender, and initially my reaction was very similar to the rich man's in Mark's gospel.

My own encounter began when a man from a local church parish came to my school in early March of 2010. He worked for the pastor of his church and was there vetting me as a possible speaker for their parishioners.

I suggested that our conversation could take place

in the school's chapel. I couldn't think of a better place to have that discussion than next to the Eucharist within the tabernacle. Seeing a student in prayer in front of the tabernacle, the visitor seemed uncomfortable talking in the chapel.

"Are you sure you want to speak in here, that it's a good place to talk?"

I assured him it was okay as long as we kept our voices down.

"Do you believe in Rome?" he asked, to my surprise.

"I'm a Roman Catholic. Of course, I do," I replied.

A bit perturbed, I wondered why he would ask me such a question. I was a pro-life speaker, Ashley and I had chosen life for our baby when 80 percent of the couples in our situation had not, and we had just endured more heartache in five months than many people do in a lifetime.

In a firm, somewhat judgmental tone of voice, the man asked:

"Do you and your wife use artificial contraception?"

Silence filled the room. I was shocked. Then I got angry. Who did this guy think he was? He had no right to judge my behavior; he did not live my life or understand my circumstances. I had been sitting at a table with men in a prayer group for several years sharing some of the most intimate details of our lives, and we would never have asked one another something like that. This guy had known me for less than five minutes!

"That's none of your business and has nothing to do with my presentation!" I replied curtly.

Noticeably offended, he began to exit the chapel.

"Well, that's about all I need to know," he said.

It appeared the conversation was over. However, I stopped him, and we finished our visit in a calm and objective way.

That day I learned – or re-learned – a valuable lesson: God always meets us where we are in our journey of life; and even in our sin, He loves us too much to leave us there. However, when it is our own sin being scrutinized, it is very difficult to see this clearly.

It took the rest of the day to re-compose myself and try to finish teaching. What had unnerved me and blown me out of my comfort zone was the man's invasive question:

"Do you and your wife use artificial contraception?"

This bothered my conscience and continued replaying over and over again in my mind. Actually, the unresolved issue burdened me for the next few months. During this time, I came across the Gospel passage about the rich man who encountered Jesus. The more I prayed about it, the more my eyes were opened. It's as though my conversation in the chapel was not with a man sent by his pastor, but with Jesus himself. Like the rich man in the Gospel, I approached Jesus in faith, longing to be closer to Him. His answer stung me.

Up until that point, I had been clinging to the one thing that was keeping Jesus from being the absolute center of our marriage: artificial contraception.

Chapter 7

Opening our minds to Natural Family Planning

I n May of 2012, my men's prayer group gathered for a final time during the school year. We were asked a series of hypothetical questions and challenged to answer them in a spiritual context.

The first question was an easy one: *If happiness were the measure of financial success, what would you do for a living?* Teaching is surely one of the most rewarding occupations, but if given the opportunity I would travel the country sharing Eli's story because it has been the most fulfilling thing I have ever done.

The second question was one that could have been answered in any number of ways: *If you could change one thing in your life, what would it be?* My answer: I would not have waited nearly seven years into our marriage to implement the Church's teaching on Natural Family Planning (NFP); I would have done it immediately.

Following my unexpected encounter with the pastor's emissary in the chapel at St. Thomas More, I opened the door to a subject that I previously wanted no part of. Ashley and I had been introduced to the concept of NFP years earlier, at our Marriage Encounter – a weekend retreat that engaged Catholic couples are required to attend before getting married.

The presentation was a complete turn-off.

A married couple walked in with a bunch of children and spoke briefly about NFP while trying to get several toddlers under control.

Glancing around the room, I noticed I was not the only guy squirming in his seat. Based on the expressions on the faces of most of the other men, it was clear we all felt the same way: uncomfortable.

Presenting NFP in this somewhat chaotic environment simply was not an effective way of convincing a skeptical audience to adopt this practice. The woman was a stay-at-home mom and her husband worked in a lucrative profession.

My initial thoughts: *This is great for couples in a high-income household, but unrealistic for a middle-class family who may not have the financial means to care for a large family.*

Had this couple made it clear how NFP had enriched their marriage as well as explained the relative ease of implementing it, I believe everyone in the audience would have been intrigued and interested in hearing more about it.

* * *

Now that I have learned more on the subject, I realize there are four things the couple could have added to their presentation to make it more convincing.

First, they could have stressed that although the Catholic Church is opposed to artificial contraception for moral and theological reasons, it does endorse a method that helps couples to plan their families. It's a process that involves a mutual commitment while fostering constant communication and trust between the two of them. It could have been pointed out that the natural biological design of the female body produces regular changes which help to accurately forecast monthly ovulation.

Second, they could have noted that couples who chose to implement this method in their marriage have been proven to either achieve or postpone a desired pregnancy 99 percent of the time.

Third, a priest or deacon should follow up by both clarifying and sharing key concepts found in Pope Paul VI's encyclical, *Humanae Vitae*, which deals with sexuality and procreation.

Fourth, modern studies have shown that couples who practice NFP have a less than two percent chance of divorce. It's a naturally designed life insurance policy on one's marriage!

These four selling points could have opened a mind and heart that was as closed as mine was at the time. I was not open to a large family and felt that our salaries would never provide the means necessary to support one. I was entering my first year teaching at a parochial school and Ashley was working as a nurse in a local hospital.

Despite Ashley's interest in learning more about NFP, I had rejected it without a second thought.

*   *   *

Even with the lingering effect of that unpleasant experience with our introduction to NFP, I began to watch programs that dealt with the topic on EWTN (Eternal Word Television Network), the global Catholic network. The more I opened my heart and mind to the teaching the more convinced I became.

Some spiritual readings also influenced this transition, such as books written by Scott Hahn, a professor at Franciscan University in Steubenville, Ohio. One of his books, *First Comes Love*, reinforced and expounded on the principles of Pope John Paul II's *Theology of the Body*.

Feeling called to initiate this change to NFP, I began seeking out more specific information on the subject. I stumbled upon a website called the Couple to Couple League. It contained personal testimonies of married couples who had begun their journey to NFP under similar circumstances as ours.

I could relate to everything they were saying; these were the most powerful personal witnesses on the rejection of artificial contraception I had ever read. They pointed out that NFP has no harmful side effects for the woman, unlike the birth-control pill, which if taken over a five-year period prior to age 30 and a first pregnancy significantly increases a woman's risk of breast cancer, cervical cancer, heart attack, stroke, and other health problems.

This information was later confirmed by my wife's OB-GYN. A devout Roman Catholic and immigrant to south Louisiana, Dr. Damon Cudihy is a fellow pro-life speaker and instructor in the Billings Method, a model of Natural Family Planning that he recommends to his patients.

"Even if the Church for some random reason would decide to change its teaching on artificial contraception tomorrow, as a practicing physician I would not prescribe it to any of my patients because I believe it's bad medicine for women," Dr. Cudihy explains.

*   *   *

Ashley and I began using NFP in the summer of 2010, about the same time we learned Eli would have to be catheterized every day, five times a day. We had been discerning for months whether to reject artificial contraception, but with our eyes now being open, it was clear the time had arrived. Eli was about 18 months old then.

The switch to NFP was a sacrificial offering, in solidarity with our son and the new burden he would have to bear for the rest of his life.

Since that time, our marriage has grown stronger and stronger. This newfound level of unity has nourished us in good times and bad. And through it all, our marriage has become what I believe God always intended it to be. More and more, we see our union as a true sacrament, that is, an outward sign of a spiritual reality, instituted by Christ to give us grace in our journey through life together.

Chapter 8

Who's the impaired one here, anyway?

In the final months of May 2011, I was engaged in a conversation with my close friend, John Listi, the Campus Minister at STM. After working with him for nearly seven years, a feeling of sadness was setting in as I realized his time at our school was coming to an end.

"Chad, what I have learned as Campus Minister is that we must never be so anxious to *serve* the Lord that we forget to *seek* Him," John said.

These words would take on a profound relevance to me in coming months and years. I reflected on them often as I continued seeking the Lord while doing my best to serve Him.

In the first two years after Eli's birth, I was engaging in public ministry and speaking to people every chance I got. I didn't realize it at the time, but I was running away from frustration and harboring a lot of anger. I wasn't ready to acknowledge it, and I surely wasn't ready to address it.

But I was at a place in my teaching career that I felt a deep desire to give back to the STM community, which had given so much to me over the years.

Motivated by this desire, I volunteered to lead the most intense retreat offered to our faculty and students. It's called *Kairos*, meaning "on God's time." It involved forming 12 seniors to minister to the upperclassmen of the student body at four weekend retreats at a camp in central Louisiana. As I prepared myself to take on this responsibility, it became evident to me that I had a great deal of work to do on myself before I could effectively lead young men and women in this retreat. I would have to deal with my own brokenness involving perfectionism and control issues, i.e., the psychological need to be in control of things all the time.

Assisting me with my own personal stuff was a priest whom I held in high regard, Fr. Joe Breaux. He helped me to take a long, hard look at myself.

We began with the first step in a well-established technique of self-examination: asking and answering the question, *Who am I?* The answer is found in the four basic needs common to all humanity. As humans, we all need:

- To receive and give love

- To feel some sort of worth or value
- To feel we belong to someone or something
- To have personal autonomy – something that makes us unique

As I reflected on this question, I was reminded that my own brokenness had always been wrapped up in my pursuit of the elusive perfection and control. Early in life, I somehow came to the illogical conclusion that unless I was perfect physically and intellectually, then I was not lovable. This perception paved the way for obsessive-compulsive behavior in just about everything I attempted. I fooled myself into thinking this type of perfectionistic behavior was a measure of my worth as a person. I guess I figured I was defined by what I did and how well I did it. My relevance and purpose were wrapped up in what I was capable of producing and consuming.

Throughout my teenage years and into my twenties I had an obsession with physical fitness that became both a blessing and a curse. I took care of my body because I thought of it as an outward manifestation of the self-discipline and value that lived within. I must have thought that it signaled to others that they were in the presence of a successful person.

I still value physical fitness today, but for a completely different reason: the ability to serve a little boy in a wheelchair, who at times is not capable of doing for himself.

As I matured, I realized it would be impossible to

recognize God's life within me without first identifying those things that blinded me to His presence. Without pursuing self-knowledge I could avoid asking myself the tough questions that would bring my faults and failures to the surface – so that I could deal with them. I had to face myself, stand naked before the Lord and ask Him two basic though profound questions: *Who am I to You? Who are You to me?*

A month before the first scheduled *Kairos* retreat, Fr. Joe and I had a brutally frank discussion about what was bothering me. This exchange occured while I was making a confession, availing myself of the graces of the Sacrament of Reconciliation.

"Are you mad or frustrated with God? If you are, it's okay. You can tell Him. He's a big boy and He can take it," Fr. Joe said.

"Yes, I am," I said, with tears rolling down my face. Surrendering further control of my emotions, I continued:

"Why didn't He heal Eli? I have died to myself for those I love the most. I have changed my whole life. I have done everything right," I sobbed.

As soon as those last words rolled off my tongue something profound settled into my consciousness: Eli is one of the happiest people I know. His physical impairments have not robbed him of his enjoyment of life. But my failure to acknowledge the frustration and disappointments I was feeling on this journey with Eli had robbed me of mine.

(Continued)

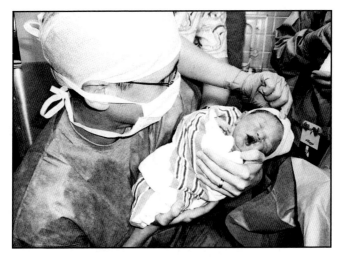

Eli was born on February 17, 2009, by Caesarean section and showed classic signs of spina bifida. *I got to hold him for a short time before he was taken to the Neonatal Intensive Care Unit. A couple days later, he underwent the first of several surgeries.*

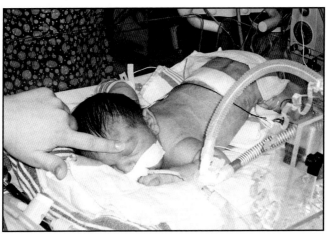

– Photo by Brad Kemp, UL-Lafayette Sports Information Dept.

For Eli's fourth birthday, on February 17, 2013, we went out to Cajun Field to play pitch-and-catch with members of the University of Louisiana at Lafayette baseball team.

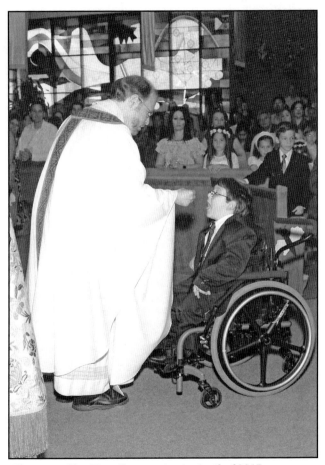

Eli received his First Communion in April of 2017 at age eight. Fr. Steve LeBlanc did the honors at St. Pius X Catholic Church in Lafayette, La.

Our third son, Ezra Matthew Judice, was baptized in August of 2014 at St. Pius X Catholic Church in Lafayette, La. Pausing for a photo with our family is my spiritual advisor, Fr. Matthew Higginbotham. Ezra got his middle name from Fr. Matthew.

Cardinal Sean O'Malley, Archbishop of Boston, takes time for a picture with Ashley, me and Jason Evert (right), a nationally known speaker on the virtue of chastity. We three men spoke about chastity and the sacredness of all human life to Boston area Catholic school students on a program titled "Created for Love." The October 2017 event was sponsored by the Archdiocese of Boston Respect Life Education Office.

2010

In 2010, our family consisted of the four of us: Ashley, me, Ephraim (pointing his finger) and Eli. Three years later (bottom photo), we were still four. The gentleman with us is Richard Malone, Bishop of Buffalo, who attended a presentation I made in Washington, D.C., in connection with the 2013 March for Life.

2013

2016

Our family grew to five with the addition of Ezra, who was born in July of 2014. In 2016, we posed with a statue of the Blessed Mother, the patroness of our family, at a church near our home.

2017

Our family in 2017 – At the time, Ezra was 3, Eli was 8, Ephraim was 12, and Ashley and I were both 39.

That session with Fr. Joe did wonders for me, psychologically and spiritually. I had remained trapped in a prison of my own making for far too long.

Upon reflection, I came to realize that perhaps the issue all along had not been so much Eli's physical paralysis as it had been my spiritual and psychological paralysis.

Eli holds on to his older brother, Ephraim – his buddy, playmate and frequent companion.

Chapter 9

Eli's big brother: a kind, gentle soul

When Eli was two years old, Ashley and I observed with great interest the development of a loving relationship between him and his older brother, Ephraim. We were – and are today – especially grateful to see the compassion and consideration shown by Ephraim toward Eli, and vice versa.

One quiet night in the autumn of 2011, when Ephraim was six years old and Eli was two, Ashley and I were sitting in the living room having a leisurely chat after putting the boys to bed. We heard a ruffling of the sheets and the pitter patter of footsteps heading our way from down the hall.

Wiping tears from his eyes, Ephraim ran into Ashley's arms. We assumed he had had a nightmare and was in need of reassurance that everything was okay.

"Buddy, what's wrong?" I asked.

"I want Eli to walk!" Ephraim replied.

Since that unforgettable moment, on numerous occasions I have found Ephraim lifting Eli from underneath his arms off the ground. Eli's otherwise motionless legs swing back and forth in mid-air as Ephraim carefully carries him forward. Ephraim's head is turned slightly over his shoulder and he's wearing a big, big smile.

"Look, Dad, Eli's walking!" Ephraim says.

These boys have played well together since early on – in the den, in the back yard, at the beach. Ephraim never excludes his brother from activities when he has friends over. He is keenly aware of the frustration Eli feels because of his physical limitations.

Though Eli is wheelchair-bound, this has never been a deterrent to his mingling with other children. The boy likes to play! And his big brother always lets him know that he wants him around.

One summer, when Eli was three and Ephraim was seven, we were at the beach in Alabama for a family vacation – Ashley and I and the boys, plus my parents. The boys were playing in our hotel room after lunch, anxiously awaiting the time to go outside again to play in the sand and surf.

Ephraim noticed that there was one chocolate chip cookie remaining in the pack. He grabbed it and lifted it toward his mouth, then stopped (rather dramatically). He broke it in half and gave a half to Eli, who proceeded to scarf it down (also in dramatic fashion).

I've heard it said countless times over the years that "the child is father to the man." And, truthfully, I believe I've learned as much from my child Ephraim as he's learned from me – particularly about being patient, considerate and compassionate. Needless to say, this makes his mother and me very proud.

Chapter 10

Whispers of a third child

I could hear the voice of the presenter at the school assembly echoing off the walls of the gymnasium. I was staring off into space anticipating an important text message from Ashley. It was late April of 2012, and I was monitoring the behavior of my students, but my mind was a thousand miles away.

Ashley was at an emergency appointment with her OB-GYN. Being late for her monthly period, having tested positive on a pregnancy test, and experiencing severe cramping, she was convinced she was having a miscarriage.

The text message popped up: It wasn't a miscarriage; she wasn't pregnant.

After practicing Natural Family Planning for a year and a half without anything like this ever happening, this unexpected episode was quite unsettling.

Later that evening, Ashley stood looking at herself in our bathroom mirror with her hands on her belly. The emotional roller coaster of the previous few days had taken a toll on her that was plain to see.

"I never knew how badly I wanted the child I didn't have," she said through tears.

I carried Ashley's words into prayer in the chapel at St. Thomas More each day moving forward, as I contemplated our having another child. At the same time, I was seriously considering changing careers, from teacher to fulltime writer and public speaker.

However, such a career change would have created other issues, such as a lack of guaranteed salary and the need to line up additional help at home to meet Eli's physical and medical needs while I would be on the road.

As time went on, our preconceived image of our family of four was not so clear anymore. Earlier in our marriage, when planning our future, we had agreed to have a child, maybe two at the most. Our initial contraceptive mentality gradually evolved into the idea that there was nothing wrong with Ashley's having her ovarian tubes tied or my having a vasectomy following the birth of our second child.

However, after thorough discussions with Ashley and an extended period of discernment, we set a realistic timeline – in the distant future – to have a third child.

But God had other plans.

* * *

In the spring of 2013, Eli experienced a number of severe and more frequent seizures due to epilepsy. My mother-in-law, Ann, was at our house helping us care for Eli and was giving him a bath. Eli, who was four at the time, turned to her and said:

"Grammy, I have a secret."

She was caught a bit off guard, but then played along.

"Really, what is it?" she replied.

"Momma is going to have a baby this year," Eli declared with certainty.

He then went back to playing in the water. Ann was more than surprised by Eli's pronouncement because she knew we would never discuss having a third child in the presence of either Ephraim or Eli.

As the summer of 2013 came to a close, I had a lot on my plate and even more on my mind. I began my ninth year teaching at St. Thomas More. I had scheduled several speaking events across the country for the upcoming school year – including one as a guest speaker for the Archdiocese of Washington, D.C., for the 41st annual March for Life in D.C. And I was still actively considering a career change.

In early October, I had the chance to visit Wichita, Kansas, as the keynote speaker for a pro-life confer-

Eli seems to be "Mr. Popularity" as he is surrounded by students from Sacred Heart High School of Ville Platte, La., in September of 2012. I gave a talk there that day and was accompanied by both my sons and my wife, Ashley.

ence. Upon completing my presentation, I invited the audience to ask questions if they'd like. I frequently get asked the same one – and I heard it again.

"Do you think you and your wife will ever have any more children?"

"We have been discerning it. We're always open to life, and although we faithfully practice Natural Family Planning, we're not actively trying to conceive at the moment. But, hey! There's always that one percent chance, right?" I responded.

A month later, Ashley was getting herself ready to attend an event for a coworker and putting on the last touches of her makeup. She hugged Eli and was telling him good-bye.

"Mommy, where are you going tonight?" he asked.

"I'm going to a baby shower for a friend from work," she replied.

Eli reached out and placed his hand on her belly.

"Mommy, you have a baby in your belly," he said.

Ashley wasn't expecting those words to come out of his mouth. There had been no announcement of any additional children on their way.

*　　*　　*

It was close to 6 a.m. on a Friday morning in November. I was rushing in from a routine workout and heading for the shower. In just a few hours, I would be hopping on a flight to Dallas for a speaking engagement that evening. Passing Ashley en route to the bathroom, I asked her what I had been asking her for the past few months.

"Did you start yet?"

Appearing to want to avoid the subject, she glided past me.

"Not yet!"

Noticing the nonchalance of her response, I pressed for a little clarity. I approached her a second time. A familiar feeling was brewing in the pit of my stomach.

"Ashley, what's going on?"

"Do you really want to have this conversation right now?" she asked in a somewhat irritated tone.

"Yeah, I do!" I replied kind of halfheartedly.

She hesitated for a moment, then smiled broadly.

"I'm pregnant!"

Chapter 11

Our Lady of Mt. Carmel, pray for us!

F rom the beginning of Ashley's third pregnancy, it was clear that there would be nothing easy about it. During her second trimester, she contracted walking pneumonia while simultaneously experiencing signs of what appeared to be the onset of a miscarriage.

An ultrasound ordered by her OB-GYN put her initial fears to rest. She had a condition that required temporary bed rest and refraining from any heavy lifting. She followed the doctor's orders, but never fully regained her health, as she battled walking pneumonia two more times before the delivery date.

In the early months of Ashley's pregnancy, I found myself in an odd, uncomfortable place. Uncertainty was all around. I continued to pray for guidance and to deal with life one day at a time.

Meanwhile, I had lost my enthusiasm for teaching what I was being paid to teach: civics and American history. I really wanted to teach theology and to share the Catholic faith. I was quite frustrated that I wasn't able to do so, and my frustration was overflowing to my home life.

By December of 2013, it appeared the immediate crisis with Ashley's pregnancy had passed and that our unborn baby was growing at a normal pace. My constant prayer was for a healthy child. Ashley's OB-GYN determined that since Ashley had had a high-risk pregnancy before and had been guided by a maternal fetal specialist in that process, the same would be necessary this time around, as a precaution.

The first four months of the pregnancy were daunting for both Ashley and me. The excitement over having a new child was tempered by the haunting memory of the ultrasound that had revealed Eli's condition *in utero* nearly five years earlier. Ashley's doctor had told her the new baby would have to be delivered by C-section, so she choose a mid-July date for the procedure. About that time, I received something from my mother-in-law that I would cling to in prayer for the duration of the pregnancy: a holy card with a prayer to Our Lady of Mt. Carmel. I would pray it daily for the health of Ashley and the new arrival to our family.

*   *   *

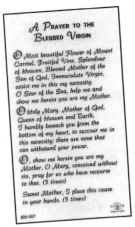

Holy card with prayer to Our Lady of Mt. Carmel that I've prayed countless times seeking Our Lady's intercession and consolation...

It was a cold day in late January 2014. I had just returned from speaking in Washington, D.C., for the March for Life. Ashley had gone for her 20-week ultrasound. I was grasping the prayer card, rubbing it nervously, when my phone rang. Ashley was on her way to school to meet me and to deliver the long-awaited news. *Was the baby okay? Was it healthy?* My heart pounded as I walked from my classroom to the front of school to meet her. She got out of the car and was holding a series of ultrasound images. Tears were running down her face.

"Everything is great, his spine is beautiful, and it's a boy!" she said.

I was extremely relieved and more than happy to hear the good news.

We had been tossing around names and had settled on one for a girl, but were unsettled on one for a boy.

"Let's name him Ezra Matthew Judice," Ashley said.

I readily agreed, and we now had a name to place in that daily prayer for mother and child.

Over the next few months I prayed hard for clarity and purpose for my future and that of my family. I was again seriously considering a life-changing decision: Do I leave teaching, or do I stay? Leaving education and becoming a fulltime speaker and author was a dream I believed could come true. I had worked vigorously to set up enough speaking engagements and saved enough money to maintain this effort for about a year.

If it didn't work out, then I always had my degree and 13 years of classroom experience to fall back on. And I knew that if I didn't give it a try I might spend the rest of my life regretting it, wondering what could have been.

So, after five years of prayerful discernment, and a place of certainty in my heart, I did something I never thought I would do: I declined an opportunity to return to teaching at STM the following school year. Talk about a leap of faith!

Initially, it appeared I had made the right decision. While on the road giving a talk, I received a call from a booking agent from a speaker's bureau – a person who represented all the Catholic speakers

I had learned from, listened to and hoped to model myself after. This lady was interested in representing me and booking me for talks all around the country. I returned home bubbling with enthusiasm about the future.

However, what followed was not what I expected. Despite the agent's best efforts, I slowly lost many of the events I had previously booked – and I could not find enough new ones to replace them. Nothing that had been successful in the past in securing these bookings was working.

I panicked. I had trouble sleeping. *How would I feed my family?* I was overcome with anxiety.

This crushing reality led me back to the last place I expected to be: I needed a job, and I needed one fast.

*   *   *

In a desperate place, with Easter approaching, I reached out to my former principal, Ray Simon, who was now principal at Catholic High in nearby New Iberia, about a half-hour drive from Lafayette. Mr. Simon had been the principal at STM when Eli's story began to unfold. He was a true father figure while at STM and was sorely missed after his unexpected departure.

I inquired about the possibility of teaching theology – something I had longed to do for quite a while.

My interview took place during Holy Week. After

Our whole family attended the March for Life in Washington, D.C., in January of 2013. That's Ephraim in the foreground, Eli snoozing in his stroller, Ashley between the boys and me just behind her.

I left, I was unsure whether I would get the job. I prayed fervently through the week, including a nine-hour novena on Easter Sunday.

The following Wednesday, I got a call from Mr. Simon offering me the job – a fulltime position in the Religion Department for the 2014-15 school year!

Relieved and grateful, I also accepted an invitation to a school Mass in May. It would be a way to get a feel for the atmosphere and culture of the school community I was about to join. I knew relatively little about the history of this venerable institution.

As the liturgy came to a close, the students sang the *alma mater* and then invoked the intercession of their patron saint, Our Lady of Mt. Carmel. As their voices echoed off the gymnasium wall, I got what south Louisiana natives call the *frissons* (goosebumps) while staring down at my mother-in-law's prayer card and its familiar words for Ashley and Ezra's well-being.

> *O most beautiful Flower of Mount Carmel, Fruit-*
> *ful Vine, Splendour of Heaven, Blessed Mother of the*
> *Son of God, Immaculate Virgin, assist me in this my*
> *necessity…. O Holy Mary, Mother of God, Queen of*
> *Heaven and Earth, I humbly beseech you from the*
> *bottom of my heart, to succor me in this necessity….*

In unison, their voices proclaimed, "Our Lady of Mt. Carmel, Pray for Us!" All of my doubts and uncertainties about what God had in store for me were cleared up that day. I had been brought to this community for a reason. Apparently, my tenure in the field of education was not over.

In the summer months that followed, Ashley's second bout with walking pneumonia necessitated her return to the hospital – only two weeks before Ezra's delivery. In this same period, Eli had several unexpected seizures and ambulance visits to a local emergency room for a growing issue that would eventually lead to his sixth major surgery.

Ezra Matthew Judice was born on July 16, 2014 – on the feast day of Our Lady of Mt. Carmel.

The following month, I started the new job, at the new school, with new students, new faculty, and a new purpose. It was a destination that only a few months earlier would have been impossible for me to imagine.

Chapter 12

A companion on the journey

One evening in the summer of 2013, I was talking by phone with a priest who was pastor of a church in Crowley, La. We were working out the details for a presentation I was going to give in his parish.

We had just started talking when our conversation was interrupted.

"Chad, who are you talking to?" Ashley asked.

"Fr. Matthew Higginbotham, the priest from Crowley," I replied.

With an amazed look I had seen only once before, in the months approaching Eli's birth, Ashley said:

"I smell roses!"

She was referring to the traditional religious belief – which we both subscribe to – that the distinct smell of roses, when roses are nowhere to be seen, is a sign that the Blessed Virgin Mary is present and assisting us in our needs.

My heart skipped a beat. Chills ran up and down my spine. I stopped Fr. Matthew mid-sentence.

"Father, excuse me, tell me again, what is the name of your parish?" I asked.

"Immaculate Heart of Mary," he replied.

A few weeks earlier, I had begun praying for Jesus to send me a priest, one under the mantle of His mother, to help me on my journey. I had been walking solo in my public speaking ministry, without a spiritual advisor, for nearly two years. I had been advised several times in the past by a close friend that my ministry would require the aid of a priest. I knew that, but had never been able to find one who I thought would fit my particular needs.

Three nights after the phone conversation with Fr. Matthew, I awoke with a lot on my mind. Walking to the kitchen, I picked up my phone to check the time and saw notifications for two new e-mails sent by Fr. Matthew. I read the first one with great interest:

> As I was praying the Rosary tonight, I was wondering if you had ever heard of Blessed Herman of Reichenau. He was born with many physical handicaps, including the same one as Eli. His parents brought him to a Benedictine monastery and left him to be raised by the monks....
>
> He was somewhat of a genius in math and science

and wrote books on these subjects. He eventually lost his sight and began to write prayers, including one that we pray at the end of every Rosary: The Hail Holy Queen!

You might be interested to look him up and learn more.

Peace and Blessings
Father Matthew

Moments later, I opened that second e-mail and found a link to the biography of Blessed Herman. What I read totally captivated me. After taking it all in, I walked over to the dishwasher and began unloading the dishes. Then it hit me like a ton of bricks: I asked for a priest; he's the priest! He's the answer to my prayer. I was now convinced that what was happening was the active intercession of the Blessed Virgin Mary.

I went to my computer to compose a response.

Father Matthew:

I have been asking the Blessed Mother's intercession in finding the priest I need for spiritual direction. I know you are a busy man and may not be able to fill this request, but to not ask would be to deny what I believe was an answer to my prayer.

Father responded later that day and agreed to meet with me and my family. When he came to visit, he revealed that the night before I e-mailed him my request, he had been sitting in his adoration chapel before the Eucharist in prayer.

"As I was praying, the Lord laid upon my heart that you were going to request I be your spiritual director, and that I better have an answer for you. Imagine the confirmation of that moment the following morning reading your e-mail containing that very request," he said.

From that moment on, Fr. Matthew, affectionately known as *Padre*, has been a mainstay and a true gift in my spiritual journey. He was the first person I called in November of 2013 when Ashley announced she was pregnant with Ezra. His countless prayers, spot-on spiritual advice, bold preaching, and personal piety have been an inspiration to me.

On several occasions leading up to Ezra's birth, medical emergencies necessitated Eli's being rushed to the emergency room. Fr. Matthew's presence there and visits to our home to pray over all of us were instrumental in carrying Ashley and me through the most challenging years of our marriage. Father baptized Ezra in August of 2014. Ezra's middle name, Matthew, is in recognition of Father's friendship and the significant role he has played in our family's well-being.

He was my confessor and confidant as I wandered through the uncharted waters of leaving St. Thomas More and moving on to Catholic High in New Iberia.

His timely advice was a voice of reason in a time of uncertainty.

The mission field I was entering at Catholic High would prove to be more complex and challenging than I could have imagined. It was good to have the *Padre* as my companion on the journey.

Chapter 13

Dark night of the soul

The start of my job as a teacher at Catholic High in New Iberia in the fall of 2014 had been both trying and exhausting. Although I was extremely grateful to have been given the opportunity to teach theology, I was not enthused about the level of interest being shown by the students in my classroom.

They were a challenging group, and I'll admit they had inherited a spiritually fatigued and emotionally wounded man for a teacher. Looking back on it, I guess it would be fair to say I was living in a fog at the time, still wrestling with my desire to be a fulltime writer and speaker. But my family needed my steady paycheck. So, for now, I needed to remain a teacher.

I sincerely wondered just how many of my students were the least bit interested in the subject I was teaching. Then one day I received a message from a student that changed my outlook and lifted my spirit.

> Mr. Judice –
>
> I am trying to turn my life around in the midst of completely losing my faith. I went home and cried one night after your class because my reality was that I was not ready to admit that I had lost God. I was so mad....
>
> So if you ever see a look of confusion or anger on my face, it's not because I don't understand or am mad at you. It's because I know it's what I needed to hear.
> – Mary-Alizabeth Beaullieu

Over time, the students and I warmed up to one another. As the days and weeks ticked by, my enthusiasm for teaching returned.

With the first week of December 2014 approaching, Ashley and I were becoming anxious about two medical procedures Eli would have to endure. One was much less severe than the other, and its time was rapidly approaching. Since birth, Eli's orthopedic surgeon had planned on breaking his lower left leg below the knee and re-setting it. This would be done to facilitate the success of the physical therapy he would need throughout his life. Because of his growth pattern over the previous five years, the optimum time was now upon us. The procedure was done on December 1, 2014, and it seemed to go well.

We were anticipating a recovery time of about a month, but a setback around Christmas landed us back in the hospital. Eli's recovery took more than three months. The ordeal included an accidental fall out of his wheelchair and his leg having to be re-cast twice. Eli was then confined to bed rest for about a month, and he put on considerable weight from being completely immobile. He also suffered side effects from medication. Nearly all the gains he had made in countless physical therapy sessions for the first years of his life were lost in that three-months span. Our feelings of victory over obstacles caused by his condition were now overshadowed by disappointment and a depressing sense of defeat.

To make matters more difficult, we were facing the necessity of a very serious major brain surgery. We had delayed this operation for two years, but both Eli's neurosurgeon and neurologist had determined it was time to operate. The last time Eli had faced such a serious brain operation was over Easter weekend of 2011, when he was just two. That operation involved replacement of the shunt which had been surgically implanted in his brain a few days after his birth. The purpose of the shunt was to eliminate excess fluid on the brain and help the fluid flow to and from his spinal cord as normally as possible.

The impending brain surgery was intended to prevent the escalation of the life-threatening grand mal seizures Eli had been having for the previous four to five years. It was also intended to address the increasing weakness he was having in his arms and hands – and hopefully to reverse this trend. The doctors anticipated that the surgery would prevent the loss or further diminishment of his motor skills, upper body agility, hand grip function, and his ability to swallow.

The medical name for the condition the surgeon intended to correct is Chiari malformation; it is common in children with the most severe form of *spina bifida.* It is a structural defect in the back of the skull. It causes part of the skull to apply pressure to the cerebellum of the brain – the part that controls all the functions that could be lost if this procedure was not done. Eli's neurosurgeon would be removing a small area of the lower back half of the skull near the spinal cord as well as part of a vertebrae.

In addition to this highly invasive operation, Eli's pediatric neurologist was suggesting a separate procedure involving the implantation of a device called a Vagus Nerve Stimulator. This device would instantaneously thwart abnormal electrical activity in the brain that brings on severe seizures – much the same way a pacemaker works to re-set an irregular heartbeat in a heart patient. The device would be placed in the upper left quadrant of Eli's chest and could be magnetically swiped from the outside to send an electronic impulse to the brain at the onset of a seizure.

*   *   *

April 20-26, 2015, was the most difficult week of my life as Eli's father. I hit rock bottom. Watching him endure the pain he did that week in the ICU of Tulane-Lakeside Hospital in Metairie took me to the brink of questioning the very existence of God.

Would Eli ever be the same child again? Would he recover all the physical gains he had worked so hard to achieve in the first five years of his life? Would I ever see that joy-filled smile again? If he didn't get better, could I be the loving husband and father I was called to be?

Truly, this was my dark night of the soul.

The dryness of my prayer combined with the emptiness in my heart were only growing from the loss of the sense of God's presence in my life.

Feeling alone and abandoned, I asked, *God, are you there?*

My only consolation came from the Blessed Mother. When Eli was diagnosed with his birth defect I had turned to her seeking the comfort only she could provide. Now I ran to her again, catching a glimpse of her pain at the foot of the Cross in St. John's gospel. Mary is one of the few people who could understand the pain of a parent watching his or her child suffer and being unable to do anything about it.

Wednesday of that week I found a glimmer of hope. It took several days and attempts by hospital personnel to get Eli sitting up in his wheelchair to re-stabilize his neck muscles after the operation. He was in the most agonizing pain I had ever seen him in.

A young college student doing volunteer community service knocked on Eli's hospital door and came in to visit with him. He accompanied us into a room where there were some toys for Eli to play with; other children were in that playroom as well. I watched Eli begin to slowly bang on a drum with a stick. As he did so, a smile gradually formed on his face. I could feel the tears running down mine. It did my heart good to see my son smiling, even though it wasn't his biggest, broadest smile.

On Friday, April 24, 2015, only four days after Eli's major surgery, I was back in Lafayette standing before a crowd of the Catholic Daughters of Louisiana, sharing Eli's story at their

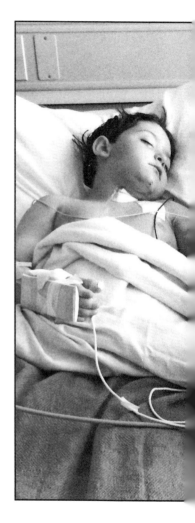

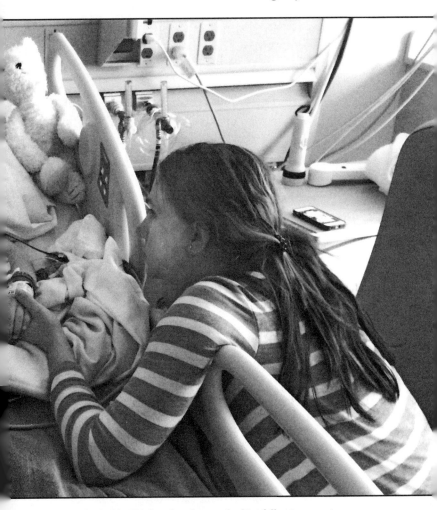

Ashley holds Eli's hand and prays for him following a serious brain surgery at Tulane-Lakeside Hospital in Metairie, La., in April of 2015.

state convention. It was one of the strongest presentations I had ever given. The thought of Eli beating on that drum gave me great energy and motivated me at a very deep level.

Early the next morning, I drove back to the hospital in Metairie to pick up Eli and Ashley. Eli was still in terrible pain. Ashley held his head steady while he sat up in the car seat on the two and a half hour drive home to Lafayette.

*   *   *

Desperate to see Eli out of pain, I reached out to a priest who had played an on-going role in Eli's life since his diagnosis *in utero*. Father Manny Fernandez is a healing priest in the Diocese of Lafayette. He came to Metairie in April of 2011 after Eli's second shunt operation, and despite his busy schedule he has always made time for Eli in emergency situations.

He came to our home the day after we returned to Lafayette. Ashley was at work, but my parents and my mother-in-law were there. Placing his hand on the back of Eli's head, Fr. Manny beckoned us to join in a prayer to the Holy Spirit for healing. Afterward, he said:

"Let's give God glory and thanksgiving for the healing."

We all prayed an additional Our Father and a Hail Mary. Then he proceeded to individually bless each

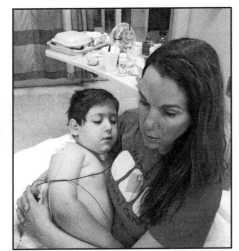

Ashley cradles Eli while he is recovering from surgery in April of 2015.

one of us. He laid his hands on my forehead, and I could feel myself starting to come out of the awful darkness that had engulfed me.

I was back at work on Monday after being gone for a week. I was trying to get my class back in order to prepare for finals when Ashley sent me a text message.

"What do you think is on Eli's head? Is it just the light from the picture? Or is it because of Father?" the message read.

The text included a picture Ashley took that morning of Eli's incision on the back of his head. There, sitting in the lower left-hand corner of the incision, was an image of the fire of the Holy Spirit. I have another photograph of Fr. Manny with an identical image on his forehead. It was taken on a pilgrimage when he was consecrating the host while celebrating Mass. I see this image as a sign of the interactive God who had broken through the confines of time and space.

When I saw this image again in Ashley's text, I knew Eli was going to be okay. And this meant I was going to be okay. From that day forward, Eli began getting better and made a full recovery in the months that followed.

*   *   *

Completely exhausted and running on grace alone, I finished the last few weeks of school and closed out my first year at Catholic High. But the doubts I had about continuing to teach wouldn't go away. That is, until an e-mail from a student after her final exams confirmed in reality what I had known all along.

Mr. Judice,

I just wanted to thank you for everything you have done this year. You have taught me so much. I am truly grateful because you have deepened my faith.

Before this year, religion had always been "Jesus loves you" with rainbows and butterflies. You have showed me how deep our Catholic faith really is and that Jesus wasn't someone who just stood by and talked about love. He told people the truth, even if it was hard to hear.

I have come to understand what St. Paul says often in his letters: Conversion is a life-long process.

Thank you for putting me on the right path and giving me the push I needed.

– Grace O'Brien

This much-needed reassurance of God's presence in my life was like a breath of fresh air. This was just the first of many affirmations to come that would light my path into the future. And that path would eventually lead me back to the place I've come to understand is home.

Chapter 14

A divine appointment on Highway 90

I always prayed and meditated while on my routine commute from home to work in New Iberia. It wasn't unusual for me to close my eyes momentarily to contemplate a mystery of the Rosary.

I had done so a thousand times, without incident.

But one day, after closing my eyes briefly, I opened them and saw, maybe 10 or 15 yards in front of me, an 18-wheeler that appeared to be either stopped or moving very slowly.

An adrenaline rush like I'd never experienced before shot through my body. Slamming on my brakes and bracing for impact, I felt my front end fold as it rammed into the vehicle in front of me. My airbag should have inflated, but it didn't. Miraculously, I wasn't hurt.

Startled and embarrassed, I pulled off the road and stopped. I got out of my vehicle to check on the other driver and to apologize.

A man in his mid-twenties got out of the truck. I was expecting him to be really upset, but that was not the case.

"Sir, I'm so sorry. Are you OK?" he said.

I was puzzled, because I knew I was in the wrong.

"No, no, I'm sorry," I said. "I was praying and for a moment I closed my eyes, and when I opened them there you were. This was my fault, not yours," I said.

I could see him processing what I had just said about praying while driving.

Then he walked around my car, giving it the once-over to see the extent of the damage. He noticed my bumper sticker that said "Pray the Rosary." That really got his attention, for reasons I didn't understand at the time.

"Are you Catholic?" he asked.

"Yes, I teach theology at Catholic High in New Iberia. I was on my way to work," I replied.

"Sir, I think you were *supposed* to hit me," he said, to my surprise.

Before I could respond to such an odd, unexpected comment, the police showed up and our conversation ended. After getting my ticket, I gave the truck driver my name and contact information.

For the rest of the day, I was in a daze, thinking I could have been killed – and reflecting on the nature of our most unusual conversation. The day after the incident, I got a message from the guy on my iPhone.

Mr. Judice –

I'm the truck driver you were in an accident with yesterday morning. Praise be to God that nobody was injured.

I'm terribly sorry about your car, and whatever other burden the incident has placed on you and your family. But I want to let you in on how this whole thing appears through my eyes.

It impacted me in a way (pun acknowledged, but not intended) that I feel I may not fully realize yet. I'm basically reading my way into the Catholic Church (through the RCIA program).... I'm also dealing with some personal struggles in my relationship with my girlfriend, who is Catholic. Our relationship spurred my initial step to begin the RCIA program. I've felt a bit confused over the past week, and began to have questions as to whether or not I was doing the right thing by joining the Catholic Church.

All those doubts came to an end yesterday when you ran into me. I'm really at a loss for words. Of all the people I could have possibly been in a crash with, it was a person who is in so many unique ways much like others who have led me into the Church through their works (Scott Hahn, Peter Kreeft, Tim Staples, etc). They've written faith-based books, appeared on EWTN, teach theology, and are Catholic....

If this isn't a divine act, then I don't suppose they happen. I know I'm on the right track now.

I've ordered your books. I'm convinced God has something in store for me in your writings....

– Frank Pellerin

Sometimes affirmations from above come over long periods of time; other times they are immediate. Things similar to this have happened several times in my life since Eli's birth.

Frank and I began having periodic exchanges on social media, including a letter from him describing the positive impact my books were having on his life.

In one of his letters, he reiterated the main thing we agreed on about what happened that day on Highway 90:

"I will forever regard our encounter as a sign from God that I am on the right track."

Call it a sign, a little miracle, or a divine appointment – but don't call it a coincidence. I, for one, no longer believe in coincidences.

Chapter 15

Miriam's Song

Ashley and I have received a lot of positive feed-back over the years in response to our decision to reject abortion, trust in God's providence, and welcome our special-needs son into the world. We have earnestly tried to be instruments of God's peace, bringing faith where there was doubt and light where there was darkness, as the prayer says.

People from all across the nation have written us to say "Thank you" for sharing Eli's story. But few let-ters have touched us as deeply as the two we received from a Medford, Wisconsin, mother whose baby was diagnosed *in utero* with a birth defect that carries with it a truly dismal prognosis.

I had spoken in her hometown in the autumn of 2016. She was moved by the pro-life, pro-faith message

I delivered while describing the impact Eli's life has had on our family and our faith.

> *Hello Chad,*
>
> *You may or may not remember me. We met when you spoke last October in Medford. I am the adviser for our Teens 4 Life group here and brought three teens to help out and see you That day was very important for all of us and we learned so much. I thank you for your trouble and ministry to us.*
>
> *But I am contacting you for an urgent prayer request and some moral support for my own family. We are pregnant with our living twelfth child. I am 15 weeks along, and through an ultrasound it was discovered the baby has anencephaly.*
>
> *It has been very hard to think of all that God has in store for us, but we do know that it is in God's hands.... It will be a hard journey, but God has given me such an overwhelming sense of peace and joy in the suffering that I almost look crazy to those who don't know me.*
>
> *I do plan on not wasting this gift that God has bestowed on us. I told my husband that we have been very actively pro-life and everyone can see that, but this might be our true pro-life story we are called to proclaim....*
>
> *What pro-abortion person isn't going to look at me, 42 with 11 kids, and think, "Why doesn't she just end it now? End her suffering and her baby's suffering.*

She needs to be there for the rest of her family."

I have already had to stand up to some of my friends who fully believe in what we like to call the "health and wealth" ministry. That is, if you just pray hard enough and believe strongly enough, God will heal your baby. Now, I truly believe He can, and that would certainly all be for His glory. But I also had to explain that that is not always God's will. And I want way more to do God's will than my own.

I also truly believe in the grace of suffering and that God has a reason for all of this. Of course, I have prayed for God to heal this baby, but I pray as Jesus did in the garden, "Let this cup pass from me; not my will but Yours be done."

It is kind of ironic, but for my last four deliveries I have taken my favorite picture of Jesus in the garden and my "mantra" was "This too shall pass" for every set of contractions. Now it has a completely different look to me. For this truly never will completely pass as those contractions did. The pain of this situation will stay with us forever, even after the baby is in heaven.

Your witness has been very close to my heart these last couple days. We are going to read your book as a family for Lent. I thank you again for all you have gone though in your life and ministry. I do keep your family in my prayers as well....

God bless you and your family,
Ann and Karl Mahner

*   *   *

Hello Chad and family –

... You were a great comforter with prayer over these past months and I so want to thank you all for that.

Miriam Grace Mahner made her beautiful appearance on Aug. 22, 2017, at 7:58 a.m. She wasn't able to move and only took a few short breaths but her heartbeat lasted for 46 minutes.

All her siblings got to hold her. But most importantly was that she was baptized, confirmed, and got last rights blessings! We had two great priests there to be with us. A nurse came into the delivery room before she was born and stated:

"There are two priests pacing in the hallway like expectant fathers!"

The whole morning was truly a blessing of sadness and grace. It is so hard to put into words.

We had her funeral and thought it would be just close family but the church was completely full. Many of those in attendance had lost babies or children. I always knew Miriam was not just here for us but for many others as well. The funeral was said by many to be the most beautiful funeral they ever attended.

My husband was the official funeral director, so that was so special for him. He got to plan the Mass and burial. The music was sung by our older children and many of our diocesan choral members.

Karl leaned to me at the end of Mass and asked

about pallbearers and, of course, I replied:

"I carried her for 9 months. I will carry her to the end."

The cemetery is directly across the road from the church, so Karl, with broken ribs, and I carried her in her little coffin to the grave site.

God's grace was so abundant you could feel it everywhere.

Although I was hoping for more time with her, it was exactly perfect and ordained by God through the whole journey. I know my physical journey of carrying her is at an end but I hope this is not the end of her story. And it is not the end of us carrying her story to others, for sure.

Please continue to pray for us when you can. And our suffering will be offered for you as well.... Again, we thank you from the depths of our souls.

May God grant you peace and hope!

Ann & Karl Mahner & Family

Chapter 16

The circle of life

I pulled into the teacher's parking lot at Catholic High in August of 2015 for the first day of my second year of teaching there. Initially, when I accepted the position a year earlier, my intention was to be at the school for just one year.

I was still clinging to idea that I could write and speak fulltime to support my family. In my first year at Catholic High, despite all of the issues we faced with Eli and my uncertainty about remaining in education, I had traveled to nine states in nine months sharing Eli's story. However, the momentum of that speaking campaign had slowed to a trickle; I no longer had nearly as many advanced bookings as before. It was time to stop running away from the obvious: I was meant to be in a classroom and to truly embrace the profession of teaching.

Sitting in the car and finishing my morning prayers before going to my classroom, I felt a deep sense of peace as I prayed. *Jesus, I am not sure why I was brought here, but I am going to embrace everything you have to offer me. Not my will, but thy will be done.*

Moments later, I was staring at an entirely new group of students. I didn't realize it then, but this class would prove to be the most influential of any group I had ever taught. In the coming year they would be the source of my re-discovering my love of teaching.

*   *   *

Within days of the start of the year, following the dismissal bell, a former student knocked on my door. I was surprised to see him. He seemingly had been disinterested in what I was teaching for a majority of the previous school year, but when engaged he always asked some great questions. I knew he was one of the brightest students in the class.

"Hey, Chris, how are you? I'm kind of surprised to see you," I said.

"Will you sign this sheet for me to be a Campus Minister this year? Oh, and would you consider being my Confirmation sponsor?" he asked.

I was so shocked by what he said that I almost couldn't speak. Recomposing myself, I replied enthusiastically:

"You better believe it!"

"Awesome! I wrote something I am going to send you to read, if you don't mind. It's my essay for campus ministry," he pointed out.

"I look forward to reading it!" I replied.

The following day I received Chris' essay in an e-mail. As I read it, everything that had been dead inside of me with regard to teaching came back to life.

I first encountered God about a year ago. Prior to that I was an atheist.

Beginning my sophomore year, Mr. Chad Judice made a reasonable argument disproving atheism. I wrestled with the idea of a Supreme Being and the possibility of knowing Him in a personal way. Being unsure, I became agnostic.

Previously, I saw religion as something for those who were too weak to go through life by themselves. However, when Mr. Judice began to focus on the life of Jesus Christ, my agnostic views were shaken. He pointed out many prophecies in the Old Testament that Jesus fulfilled. Initially, I ignored those fulfilled prophecies because I had no answers for them....

I didn't want to live a Catholic life. I believed I didn't need God and could get through life on my own. Pride reassured my belief I could handle whatever life threw at me. And if I struggled, I had my girlfriend to help me through it. But when we broke up, I was left broken, with no one to turn to.

In fear, I suppressed my inner sorrows and almost ended it all. In a desperate attempt to keep my life, I turned to God.... Taking a leap of faith, I asked God to help me through it. After I realized He had done just that, I began to embrace all the Catholic faith had to offer from that point on.

– Christopher White

With a new fire in my heart, I began to teach the way I had earlier in my career. I was smiling, engaging my students on a personal level, and becoming a more effective minister and teacher. For the first time in a long time, I was waking up and really wanting to go to work. Finding a joy I thought was gone forever, I continued to spiritually guide Christopher all the way through to his Confirmation. Watching him enter into full union with the Church as he was anointed by the Bishop in his Confirmation was one of the most surreal moments in my teaching career. It was one thing to have helped students become productive citizens of the United States by teaching civics, but it was something on an entirely different playing field to watch my student make a commitment to become an eternal citizen of Heaven. I finally understood what St. Paul meant when he described all of us as being co-workers in Christ – instruments Christ uses to bring others to Himself.

A week after Christopher's Confirmation, I was meeting with Father Matthew for spiritual direction.

I was sharing some of Chris' story with him when the conversation turned to my future in education. Despite all the great things about Catholic High, I couldn't see being there for an extended period of time. The 40-minute drive from Lafayette was problematic in the event of an emergency involving Eli; I was just too far from home. Also, my son Ephraim would be a freshman at St. Thomas More in the next four years, and I wanted to be there for him. Father and I agreed that returning to teach at STM at some point in the future might very well be in God's plan – and in my family's best interest.

A few days after that discussion, I received an e-mail from the head of the Theology Department at St. Thomas More. The subject line stated, *Opening in STM Religion Department.*

Chad,

We have an opening in the Religion Department to teach 10th grade theology. We want to interview you. Are you interested?

*   *   *

Sitting here in May of 2017 at the close of my first year back at STM, the school where this journey began in 2005, I can clearly see God's hand in my life and that of my family. Teaching theology is more challenging; it has opened so many other doors that remaining in a civics classroom never would have. As I have continued to teach theology, I have increased in my understanding of the objective truths found in my Catholic faith.

It was in the darkness of an ultrasound room that my true conversion began. It was the realization of Eli's condition *in utero* that propelled Ashley and me to actively cooperate with the faith, hope and love we needed in order to hold up under the substantial challenges with which we were presented.

Thankfully, we found our way by the grace of God. Jesus said, "I am the way, the truth and the life. No one comes to the Father except through me." We believe this as the pure truth, for it is Jesus who sustains us on our journey through life as we continue growing with Eli.

*   *   *

In February of 2018, Eli turned nine years old. He was a second-grader at a public school in Lafayette, where his physical and medical needs were attended to by the faculty and staff.

Making music is something that has always brought joy to Eli. He now plays the piano and genuinely loves music. His skills have advanced enough for him to play in recitals. Playing music is a great way to stimulate his mind and help further develop physical dexterity in areas not impacted by his birth defect. He can play the Catholic hymn, "Immaculate Mary."

Every time he plays it, I can't hold back my tears.

I believe he will graduate from high school some day and will then have an opportunity to earn a college degree and/or develop a trade that could give him full independence. One way or the other, he will continue to battle the physical, psychological, social and emotional challenges of a special-needs person.

Ashley and I have long embraced a one-day-at-a-time approach to things – in the interest of maintaining our own well-being and sanity as his parents. We've learned through experience not to dwell too heavily on the events of the past nor to speculate much on what the future may hold. Truly, Eli has taught us how to live in the present moment, to see and appreciate the blessings that are right in front of us. These blessings help us to feel God's presence and to see how He is at work in our lives.

Eli's Chiari malformation surgery left some lingering effects on his emotional state of being. Though he is nine years old, there are times when his overly sensitive responses to routine parent-child interactions seem like those of a much younger child. However, these moments have also drawn extraordinary degrees of compassion out of Ashley and me that are a constant reminder of the privilege it is to be his parents.

Regardless of what the future holds for Eli, I believe his ability to elicit responses of compassion and love from those around him will continue to be one of his greatest gifts to the world. And because of this,

Ashley and I are optimistic for Eli's future. We are encouraged by the wisdom we find in holy scripture – that of the three theological virtues of faith, hope and love, the greatest of these is love.

Afterword

'Waiting For Eli' – *the movie?*

Eli's story has resonated with audiences all over the United States for a number of years, and now there's a chance the story may be headed for the big screen. We're working on it.

Who wouldn't be attracted to the true story of a boy, diagnosed *in utero* with *spina bifida*, whose parents choose to bring him to term rather than abort him, as 80 percent of Americans would have done after learning of such a diagnosis? And the boy, who undergoes several serious surgeries, turns out to be such a fine youngster – smart, full of personality, the very picture of life.

The talk of a movie began in 2015, shortly after film-makers Marcus and Yvette Brown of Lafayette, La., saw a video I had posted on YouTube. Titled *Eli's Reach: A Family's Journey from Fear to Faith*, the video is based on material from my first two books, *Waiting For Eli* and *Eli's Reach*.

Marcus and Yvette were quite moved by the video and contacted me to talk seriously about their making a big-screen, faith-based movie. Their company, by the way, is called Believe Entertainment.

They felt Eli's story would make a great movie. It would feature a central character everyone seems to love. And it would contain a worthwhile message our country needs to continue to hear: that unborn babies are human beings and should be welcomed into our world, irrespective of im-pairments, imperfections, or the convenience of the parents.

Needless to say, I was thrilled that the Browns saw it this way. As I've said before, when a writer is passionate about the story he wants to tell, he wants to tell the world. To have filmmakers tell it in their medium would be a welcome addition to my campaign.

The next step in our pursuit of the movie was to have a screenplay written. We found our writer in Brennan Robideaux of Lafayette, the same guy who produced the YouTube video of Eli's story. So, he went to work again and came up with a top-notch script, titled *Waiting For Eli*. I mean, it is *really* well done!

As of this writing, all we need in order to produce this film and take it to the big screen is the funding. Brennan's screenplay is inspiring, and the Browns believe the story has the power to win hearts and minds for the pro-life cause – plus, it's simply a very compelling story with an unforgettable little character.

But, like all artistic endeavors, this one needs funding. So it's our sincere hope and prayer that those in a position to back our project will come forward and offer the necessary financial support.

*   *   *

With the publishing of this, the third book in a trilogy, Eli's story is not yet over – far from it. The story continues to unfold as Eli ventures forth as an elementary school pupil. And it'll continue to be told for as long as I can find audiences who are willing to listen.

Like I said, I want to tell the world.

Appendix 1

The Rosary

Begun nearly eight hundred years ago, the Rosary can be a very beautiful form of prayer for us today. The melodious repetition of Hail Marys and Our Fathers is a chant prayer which forms the background for meditation on each of the Mysteries.

The rosary starts with the Apostles' Creed, an Our Father and three Hail Marys. Then each of five mysteries is introduced by an Our Father which is followed by ten Hail Marys. These make up each decade. While praying the decade, each one can meditate upon the ideas offered below.

Traditionally, the Joyful Mysteries are said on Monday and Thursday, the Sorrowful on Tuesday and Friday, and the Glorious on Sunday, Wednesday and Saturday.

The Joyful Mysteries

The Annunciation – to obtain humility. We consider how the Archangel Gabriel announced to Mary that she was to conceive our Blessed Lord.

The Visitation – to obtain love of neighbor. We consider Mary's visit to her cousin, Elizabeth.

The Nativity – to obtain detachment from the world. We consider the birth of our blessed Lord in a stable at Bethlehem.

The Presentation – to obtain respect for authority. We consider how Mary presented Our Lord in the temple forty days after His birth.

Finding in the Temple – to obtain love of Jesus. We consider how Mary lost her Son in the temple and found him after three days.

The Sorrowful Mysteries

The Agony in the Garden – to obtain resignation to God's will. We consider our Lord praying in the garden and sweating blood.

The Scourging at the Pillar – to obtain a spirit of purity. We consider how our Lord was whipped.

The Crowning with Thorns – to obtain moral courage. We consider how our Lord was cruelly crowned with thorns and mocked.

The Carrying of the Cross – to obtain patience in trials. We consider how our Lord was compelled to carry a heavy cross to Calvary.

The Crucifixion – to obtain sorrow for sin. We consider how our Lord was nailed to the cross, and after a three-hour agony, died.

The Glorious Mysteries

The Resurrection – to obtain an increase of faith. We consider how Jesus rose gloriously the third day after His death.

The Ascension – to obtain an increase of hope. We consider how Jesus ascended into heaven, in the presence of His mother and of His disciples.

The Descent of the Holy Spirit – to obtain an increase of love. We consider how Jesus sent the Holy Spirit on the Apostles and the Blessed Virgin.

The Assumption – to obtain devotion to Mary. We consider how the Blessed Virgin Mary, body and soul, was taken up into heaven after her death.

The Coronation – to obtain the grace of perseverance. We consider how, in heaven, Mary was crowned by her Son Queen of Angels and Saints.

The Luminous Mysteries

The Baptism of Jesus – Jesus descends into the water of the Jordan River and is baptized by John. The heavens open and the voice of the Father declares Him the beloved Son. The Spirit descends upon Jesus in the form of a dove and fills Him with God's mission to save humankind from sin.

The Wedding at Cana – Jesus changes water into wine at the request of Mary, who was first among believers. The disciples witness this miracle, their hearts open to the faith, and they begin to believe in Him.

The Proclamation of the Kingdom of God – Jesus preaches the Gospel in Galilee. He proclaims that this is the time of fulfillment, for the Kingdom of God is at hand. He asks all to repent and forgives the sins of those who believe in Him.

The Transfiguration – On Mount Tabor, the Apostles see the glory of God shining forth from the face of Jesus. The voice of the Father, coming from a cloud, says, "This is my chosen Son, listen to Him."

The Institution of the Eucharist – At the Last Supper, Jesus offers His body and blood, under the signs of bread and wine, and washes the feet of the Apostles. He knows that Judas has betrayed Him and His hour has come. Jesus testifies to His everlasting love for each one of us by sharing the Sacrament of the Eucharist.

(Source: Our Lady of the Oaks Retreat House Prayer Booklet, Grand Coteau, Louisiana)

Appendix 2

Letters of support for Eli's story

Dear Mr. Judice:

I am so glad that I attended the Pro-Life Rally at my parish, St. Matthew's Cathedral in Washington, D.C., on January 22, 2014. Your presentation prompted me to order and to read your two books, and they have fundamentally changed how I see my role.

I am a Catholic and a human rights attorney, but I have often shied away from the pro-life/pro-choice debate, regarding it as too politicized, and, at the end of the day, I could not tell another person what to do. I have represented victims of human trafficking and domestic violence, who were raped and impregnated with children and it was so painful to hear their stories.

But, through your story, I have come to realize there is a role for me in the pro-life movement and it is in my purview to advocate for the dignity of all human life, without being judgmental. Thank you for sharing your story. May God continue to bless you, Eli and the rest of your beautiful family.

– *Christina Parello*

* * *

In my junior year in high school, I was in a class called Peer Support. Students who were in regular education had the opportunity to work hands-on with students with special needs in their adapted physical education class.

I loved being a part of something so special! At the time, I was also attending confirmation classes at my church, and every Sunday night, the class would get together for an hour to listen to a guest speaker. One of those speakers, Chad Judice, came to talk to us about his son Eli and their family. I was captivated by his story; my attention never drifted. At the end of his talk, he said, "And now, I would like for you to meet my son, Eli."

Eli's mother walked into the room holding Eli in her arms, and I couldn't help but cry uncontrollably. For some unknown reason, I couldn't control my emotions.

An older lady who volunteered at the church pulled me aside and asked if I was okay. I told her that I didn't know why I was crying, but that I felt the need to meet Eli. She helped me get myself together and we went up to Eli and his parents so I could say hello. After speaking to them for a minute or two, the older lady pulled me aside again, asking me if I felt better. I told her I had this weird feeling in my stomach and I didn't know why. She then told me she thought God was trying to tell me something, and I needed to figure out what it was.

The next day my first class was my favorite class, Peer Support! The minute I walked into the classroom, and I saw those special-needs kids, I got that same feeling in my stomach that I had when I met Eli. I got a sudden rush of emotions. In that moment, I realized God was trying to tell me something: This is what I needed to do with my life – work with kids with special needs. This is why He put me on this earth. This was His plan for me.

Then I looked at those kids, and I couldn't help but smile, accepting God's plan.

Since that day, I have never forgotten Chad, his wife, and his son, Eli. They hold a special place in my heart. They have helped me figure out my future, my life, my passion – working with individuals with special needs!

I now work with the DREAMS Foundation of Acadiana, a non-profit organization whose mission is to help individuals with special needs, as well as their families. We sponsor 15 activities for people with special needs and help to educate the public on the needs and wants of our clientele.

(For more information, go to: www.dreamsfoundationaca.org.)

– *Laynie LeBlanc*
  Lafayette, La.

*   *   *

Dear Chad,

I just wanted to say thank you for writing *Waiting for Eli*. It has truly opened my eyes to what is right in front of me, as well as opened my heart to God. I am 33 years old and have a 2-year-old daughter.

After reading your book I realized how much I take my family for granted. I am blessed to have a healthy child, but I never stopped to thank God for her.

I have secretly been battling addiction and have known for quite some time that I needed help. The thought of suicide has passed through my mind numerous times. Reading your book truly has been the help that I needed. I opened my heart up to God and prayed for help. I feel like a new man and never want to go back to that dark place again. You truly have saved my life.

Thank you for sharing your story and for giving my daughter the father she deserves.

– *Eric Soileau*

*   *   *

Chad,

Thank you so much for being our guest today on *At Home with Jim and Joy Pinto.* You were outstanding! Your testimony on your son, Eli, was an awakening to the beauty and sanctity of every human life.

We look forward to having you back on the show again in the near future. We know that the story of Eli will touch and inspire many lives.

– *Mike Romano*
  EWTN Radio Producer

Sources

Books, magazine articles, and other printed documents

Catechism of the Catholic Church, with Modifications from the Editio Typica. New York: Doubleday, 1997.

Evert, Jason. *Saint John Paul the Great: His Five Loves.* Lakewood, Colo.: Totus Tuus Press, 2014.

Fisher, Simcha. *The Sinner's Guide to Natural Family Planning.* Huntington, Ind.: Our Sunday Visitor, 2014.

Gillespie, Hugh. *Preparation for Total Consecration According to Saint Louis de Montfort.* Bay Shore, N.Y.: Montfort Publications, 2001.

Hahn, Scott. *First Comes Love: Finding Your Family in the Church and the Trinity.* New York: Doubleday, 2002.

——. *Hail, Holy Queen: The Mother of God in the Word of God.* New York: Doubleday, 2001.

——. *Reasons to Believe: How to Understand, Explain, and Defend the Catholic Faith.* New York: Doubleday, 2007.

Holy Bible. New American Bible. Rev. ed. Wichita: Saint Jerome Press, 2011.

Kelly, Matthew. "Even a Blind Man Knows..." In *Rediscover Catholicism: A Spiritual Guide to Living with Passion & Purpose,* pp. 89-113. North Palm Beach, Fla.: Beacon Publishing, 2010.

Kleponis, Peter C. "God's Plan for Sexuality." In *Integrity Restored: Helping Catholic Families Win the Battle against Pornography,* pp. 265-284. Steubenville, Ohio: Emmaus Road Publishing, 2014.

Richards, Larry. *Be a Man! Becoming the Man God Created You to Be.* San Francisco: Ignatius Press, 2009.

——. *Surrender!: The Life-Changing Power of Doing God's Will.* Huntington, Ind.: Our Sunday Visitor, 2011.

Sheed, F. J. *Theology and Sanity.* 2nd ed. Huntington, Ind.:

Our Sunday Visitor, 1978.

Sheen, Fulton J. *Life of Christ.* 1958. Reprint, New York: Doubleday, 2008.

Staples, Tim. "Truth and Consequences: Without a Teaching Authority, Morals Become Relative." *Catholic Answers,* January/February 2014, pp. 24-31.

———. "Why Mary Matters: Answering Objections to the Title 'Mother of God.'" *Catholic Answers,* November/December 2014, pp. 22-27.

Vanderwall, Francis W. *Spiritual Direction: An Invitation to Abundant Life.* New York: Paulist Press, 1981.

Wall, James S. "More Pertinent than Ever: Pope Paul VI's Prophetic Encyclical Reconsidered." *Catholic Answers,* May/June 2016, pp. 14-19.

Online

"Birth Control and NFP: What's the Difference?" *Priests for Life.* June 20, 2013. http://priestsforlife.org/articles/nfpdifferences.html.

"Chiari Malformation." *Cincinnati Children's.* July 2016. https://www.cincinnatichildrens.org/health/c/chiari-malformation.

"Contraception." *Catholic Answers.* January 1, 1996. https://www.catholic.com/magazine/print-edition/contraception.

Couple to Couple League for Natural Family Planning. June 20, 2013. http://ccli.org/.

Fingerhut, Hannah. "On Abortion, persistent divides between–and within–the two parties." *Pew Research Center.* July 7, 2017. http://www.pewresearch.org/fact-tank/2017/07/07/on-abortion-persistent-divides-between-and-within-the-two-parties-2/.

Kaczor, Christopher. "Contraceptive Claims." *Catholic Answers.* February 1, 1992. https://www.catholic.com/magazine/print-edition/contraceptive-claims.

"Marriage & Divorce." *American Psychological Association.* June 20, 2013. http://www.apa.org/topics/divorce/.

"Mother Angelica, foundress of EWTN, dies on Easter." *Catholic News Agency.* March 27, 2016. https://www.catholicnewsagency.com/news/mother-angelica-founder-of-ewtn-dies-on-easter-75329.

Murphy, Caryle. "What is a sin? Catholics don't always agree with their church." *Pew Research Center.* September 25, 2015. http://www.pewresearch.org/fact-tank/2015/09/25/whats-a-sin-catholics-dont-always-agree-with-their-church/.

"Nerve Stimulation for Epilepsy." Healthwise Staff. *WebMD.* February 20, 2015. https://www.webmd.com/epilepsy/vagus-nerve-stimulator-for-epilepsy.

Newport, Frank. "Americans, including Catholics, Say Birth Control is OK Morally." *Gallup News.* May 22, 2012. http://news.gallup.com/poll/154799/americans-including-catholics-say-birth-control-morally.aspx .

Popcak, Dr. Gregory. "Sex, Lies, and the Catholic Church." *Catholic Exchange.* January 5, 2017. http://catholicexchange.com/sex-lies-catholic-church.

Pope Paul VI. "Humanae Vitae: On the Regulation of Human Birth." *Papal Encyclicals Online.* 1968. http://www.papalencyclicals.net/Paul06/p6humana.htm.

"The Position of the Church on Artificial Contraception." *American Life League.* 1931. https://www.ewtn.com/library/PROLENC/ENCYC098.HTM.

Staples, Tim. "Truth and Consequences." *Catholic Answers.* August 28, 2015. https://www.catholic.com/magazine/online-edition/truth-and-consequences.

References

p. 15 – *...called spina bifida.:* This is a neural tube defect that adversely affects the development of the baby's brain and spinal cord *in utero.* Symptoms can include bowel and bladder problems, urinary tract infections, fluid on the brain (hydrocephalus), paralysis of the lower extremities, and learning disabilities.

p. 16 – *EWTN:* The Eternal Word Television Network is a global Catholic network that presents around-the-clock Catholic-themed programming. "The largest religious media network in the world," it was founded in 1981 by Mother Angelica, a Poor Clare nun. According to EWTN's mission statement, the network is "dedicated to the advancement of truth as defined by the magisterium of the Roman Catholic Church."

p. 33 – *...Society of Jesus, the Jesuits.:* A religious congregation of the Catholic Church which originated in 16th century Spain. The Jesuits are engaged in evangelization and apostolic ministries in 112 nations on six continents, including the founding and operating of schools, colleges and seminaries. Founded by Ignatius of Loyola, Spain, the society offers Spiritual Exercises retreats around the world.

The Spiritual Exercises, held in the highest regard in the Roman Catholic Church, are a collection of spiritual activities including prayer, meditation, scriptural readings, examination of conscience, and acts of self-denial. These are designed to strengthen one's spiritual health, thus drawing the person into closer communion with God. Just as physical exercise will strengthen the muscles of the body, so too will spiritual exercise strengthen the person's spiritual life and health.

p. 44 – *Secular Franciscans (The Third Order of Saint Francis):* A community of men and women throughout the world who strive "to observe the Gospel of our Lord Jesus Christ by following the example of St. Francis of Assisi, who made Christ the inspiration and center of his life." (In Latin, it's *Ordo Franciscanus Saecularis,* or OFS.)

p. 48 – *Theology of the Body:* Pope John Paul II's teachings on love, life and human sexuality. These were given in a series of 129 lectures during the Pope's Wednesday audiences in Rome from 1979 through 1984.

p. 51 – *Do you believe in Rome?:* Translated, Do you accept the teachings and the authority of the Roman Catholic Church, as stated by the magisterium of the Church?

p. 64 – *Sacrament of Reconciliation:* Formerly referred to as Confession or the Sacrament of Penance, this is a sacrament in which the priest, as the agent of God, forgives sins on the conditions that the sinner is truly sorry for them, sincerely confesses them, and is willing to make amends for them.

p. 81 – *March for Life:* An annual rally protesting the practice and legality of abortion, held in Washington, D.C., on or around the anniversary of Roe vs. Wade, the landmark decision issued in 1973 by the U.S. Supreme Court de-criminalizing abortion. The march, whose stated purpose is "to provide all Americans with a place to testify to the beauty of life and the dignity of each human person," advocates the overturning of Roe vs. Wade.

p. 88 – *Our Lady of Mt. Carmel:* The title given to the Blessed Virgin Mary in her role as patroness of the Carmelite Order. The first Carmelites were Christian hermits living on Mount Carmel in the Holy Land during the late 12th to mid-13th century.

Since the 15th century, devotion to Our Lady of Mt. Carmel has centered on the Scapular of Our Lady of Mt. Carmel, also known as the Brown Scapular. This is a sacramental associated with promises of Mary's special aid for the salvation of the devoted wearer.

p. 91 – *Holy Week.*: The week leading up to Easter Sunday, the day of the resurrection of Jesus Christ from the dead. It includes Palm Sunday, Holy Thursday, Good Friday and Holy Saturday.

p. 95 – *"I smell roses!"* The Blessed Virgin Mary is sometimes referred to as "Our Lady of the Roses" because roses are one of her symbols. When she is present among us, we may smell roses though none seem to be near.

p. 115 – *RCIA program:* The Rite of Christian Initiation of Adults, this is a formation program for prospective converts to Catholicism.

p. 118 – *...the baby has anencephaly.* A defect marked by the absence of a major portion of the brain, skull and scalp that occurs during embryonic development. With a very few exceptions, infants with this disorder do not survive longer than a few hours after their birth.

Index

Note: Page numbers in *italics* refer to photographs or maps.

Abortion, vi, 16–19, 21, 39
Advent missions, 157
affirmations, 111, 116
agnostic views, 125
anencephaly, 118
Angers, Trent, vi–viii
Apostles' Creed (prayer), 133
Archdiocese of Boston Respect
    Life Education Office, 69
"army-crawling," vi, vii, 45
Arroyo, Raymond, 16
artificial contraception. *See*
    contraception
At Home with Jim and Joy Pinto
    (EWTN program), 16, 140
atheism, disproving, 125

Basic needs, four, 62–63
Beaullieu, Mary-Alizabeth, 102
Billings Method (Natural Family
    Planning), 59
birth control. See contraception
birth-control pill, effects on
    women, 59
birth defects, viii, 16, 38–40,
    105, 108, 117–118, 128
    see also *spina bifida*
Blessed Herman of Reichenau, 96
Blessed Virgin Mary
    and Ashley Judice, vii, 41,
      95–96
    and Chad Judice, vii, 41, 105
    Great intercessor, role as, 21, 40
    and her pain, 105
    intercession with Jesus Christ,

    40, 89, 93, 97
    as mother of Jesus, 40
    as Our Lady of Mt. Carmel,
      88, 89, 93–94
    and the Rosary, 40, *40*, 41,
      97, 133–136
    roses, smell of, and her
      presence, 95–96
    statue of, *71*
Body, Theology of the, 48
Breaux, Fr. Joe, 31, 33, 62,
    64, 73
Brown, Marcus and Yvette
    (filmmakers), 131

Cajun Field, University of
    Louisiana at Lafayette, *66*
Cathedral-Carmel School,
    Lafayette, La., ix, 23
catheterization, 39, 48
Catholic Church, ix, x, 21,
    48–50, 55–57, 115
Catholic Daughters of
    Louisiana, 106, 108
Catholic faith, vi, x, 21, 48, 88,
    110, 126, 128
Catholic High School, New
    Iberia, La., 91, 98–99, 101,
    110, 114, 123, 127
Catholic television network.
    See EWTN (Eternal Word
    Television Network)
Catholic TV, 157
chastity, virtue of, 69
Chiari malformation, 104, 129

children, x
   special-needs children, ix,
      35, 37–38, 48, 129, 137–139
coincidences, 116
confession (Sacrament of
   Reconciliation), 64
Confirmation, 44, 124–126, 138
contraception, vii, viii, 21, 48–49,
   55–60
control freak, 16
conversion, 110
Couple to Couple League (website),
   58–59
"Created for Love" (program for
   students), 69
crusade, on manning-up, ix, x
Cudihy, Dr. Damon, 59

Despair, from despair to hope, ix
divorce rate, 48, 57
DREAMS Foundation of Acadiana
   (non-profit organization), 139
dying to oneself, 33, 64

Eli's Reach: On the Value of Human
   Life and the Power of Prayer
      (Judice), vi, 19, 157
Eucharist, 51, 98, 136
Evert, Jason, 69
EWTN (Eternal Word Television
   Network), 16, 58, 115, 140

Faith, ix, x, 18–19, 21, 27, 34, 52,
   58, 88, 90, 102, 110, 115,
   117–118, 126, 128, 130,
   134–135, 157
families, x, 18, 57, 139
family planning, natural. See
   contraception
Father Matthew. See Higginbotham,
Fr. Matthew P. "Padre"

fathers
   absence of, effect on
      children, ix, x
   See also Judice, Chad
fear, ix, 19
Fernandez, Fr. Manny (healing
   priest), 108–109
four basic needs, 62–63
Franciscan University,
   Steubenville, Ohio, 58
Franciscans, Secular (Third
   Order of St. Francis), 44
frissons (goosebumps), 93

Global Catholic network.
   See EWTN (Eternal Word
   Television Network)
Glorious Mysteries, 40, 134–135
God
   asking God for help, 126
   bargaining with, 49
   to be men after God's own
      heart, x
   blessing of Chad, Eli, and
      family, 137
   dependent upon, 38
   and Eli, 18, 64, 137
   emptiness, filling by, 32
   encountering, 125
   existence of, 105
   faith in, 21, 34
   as Father, 27. See specific
      topics in this heading
   gifts from, 33
   giving all to without
      reservation, 50
   giving up on, 18
   "God, are you there?," 105
   and "God loves you," 27
   God's life within one, 64
   God's love, 27–28

God's plan, ix, 47, 81, 94, 116, 118, 121, 127, 139
  as God's servant first, 33
  God's will, saying "yes" to, viii
  grace of, 121, 128
  and healing, 64, 108, 119
  honoring of, 38
  hope, granting by, 121
  Kingdom of, 41
  and a life with more room for God, 18
  losing God, 102
  loves us too much to leave us in sin, 52
  and marriage, 24, 28, 60
  meets us where we are, 52
  and men being men after God's own heart, x
  mercy of, praying for, 39, 117
  and Miriam Grace Mahner, 118–119, 121
  in the Mysteries of the Rosary, 134–135
  needing, 125
  "on God's time" *(Kairos)*, 60
  opening heart to, 139
  peace, granting by, 121
  peace of, being instrument of, 117
  praise to, 115
  praying to, 27, 37, 39, 139
  presence of, 105, 111, 129
  providence of, trust in, 38–39, 117
  sign from, 116
  surrendering to, 49
  thanking, 44, 139
  trust in, 17, 49
  turning to, 126
  understanding of as something, not someone, 27
  wanting all Chad's love, 50
  will of, saying "yes" to, viii

See also Holy Spirit; Lord
goosebumps *(frissons)*, 93
Gospels, 33, 41–42, 105, 135
grace, ix, 33, 60, 110, 119–121, 128, 135
Great intercessor. *See* Blessed Virgin Mary
Growing with Eli: Our Journey into Life and Light (Judice), vi, viii, 157

Hahn, Scott, 58, 115
Hail Holy Queen (prayer) (Reichenau), 97
Hail Mary (prayer), 40, 108, 133
happiness, 29, 55
healing, 64, 108, 119
Henley, William Ernest, 38–39
Herman of Reichenau, Blessed, 96
Higginbotham, Fr. Matthew P. "Padre," ix, x, 68, 95–99
Holy Spirit, 108–109, 135
hope, ix, x, 105, 121, 128, 130, 134
"How choosing life changed everything" (Judice) (op-ed piece) *(New York Post)*, 16–19, 20
human life, 17, 19, 69, 137, 140
Humanae Vitae (encyclical) (Pope Paul VI), 57
hydrocephalus, 43

Immaculate Conception Catholic Church, Washington, La., x
Immaculate Heart of Mary Church, Crowley, La., 96
"Immaculate Mary" (Catholic hymn), 129–130
intercession, 21, 40, 89, 93, 97
Intercessor, great. *See* Blessed Virgin Mary

Invictus (poem) (Henley), 38–39
iron sharpens iron, vii, 34

Jesuits (Society of Jesus), 33
Jesus Christ
    approaching in faith, 52
    co-workers in Christ, 126
    conversations with, 50, 52
    friendship with, cultivating, 31
    Glorious Mysteries, 40
    intercession with by Blessed
        Virgin Mary, 40, 89, 93, 97
    and "Jesus loves you," 110
    Joyful Mysteries, 40
    life and teachings of,
        connecting to, 32, 125
    and love, 50, 110
    Luminous Mysteries, 40–41
    marriage as sacrament
        instituted by, 53, 60
    Mary, mother of Jesus. *See*
        Blessed Virgin Mary
    and men's prayer group at
        St. Thomas More Catholic
        High School, 31–34
    mother of. *See* Blessed
        Virgin Mary
    and the Mysteries of the
        Rosary, 40–41, 133–136
    Old Testament prophecies,
        fulfilling, 125
    praying in the garden, 119
    praying to, 96, 124
    and the rich man, 50, 52
    as Savior, 31
    Sorrowful Mysteries, 40
    teachings of, connecting to
        everyday life, 32
    understanding of, deepening
        of, 31
    See also Lord

John Paul II, Pope, 58
Joyful Mysteries, 40, 133–134
Judice, Ashley Guillotte
    abortion, rejection of, 17, 39
    artificial contraception,
        rejection of, vii, viii, 59
    and Blessed Virgin Mary,
        vii, 41, 95–96
    and C-sections, 43, 88
    and Catholic religion, faith,
        117–118
    and Chad (husband), 16,
        24–25, 27–28, 60, 157
    and Eli (son), viii, ix, 16–19,
        21, 38–39, 45, 88, 105,
        108, 128–130, 138, 157
    and Ephraim (son), 23–25,
        27–28, 77, 157
    and Ezra (son), 49, 68, 81,
        84–85, 87–90, 93–94, 157
    and Fr. Manny Fernandez,
        108–110
    and God, viii, 17, 28, 38–39,
        60, 117, 129
    and human life, value of
        from conception, 17
    and living in present
        moment, 129
    and the Lord, 28, 41
    and Natural Family
        Planning (NFP), 56–60, 79
    as neonatal intensive care
        nurse, 37
    as nurse in NICU, 17
    and OB-GYN, 59, 87–88
    one-day-at-a-time approach
        to things, 129
    parents of, vii, 44
    photos of, *68–72, 92–93,
        106–107, 109*
    and praying, prayers, 17, 41

pregnancies of, 16, 23–25, 27,
37–39, 43, 80–81, 84–85,
87–90
Judice, Chad
abortion, rejection of, 17, 39
about, 157
Advent missions, leading, 157
affirmations lighting path,
111, 116
and artificial contraception,
vii, viii, 49, 51–53, 59
and Ashley (wife), vii, 16,
24–25, 27–28, 60, 157
atheism, disproving, 125
and automobile accident,
113–116
and Blessed Virgin Mary, vii,
41, 105
and Catholic Church,
growing in love for the
Church, 48
and Catholic faith, vi, 21,
48, 88, 117–118, 128
and Christopher White,
124–127
as co-worker in Christ, 126
as coach, ix, 16, 23, 47
coincidences, not believing
in, 116
college degree of, 16, 157
and Confirmation, 44,
124–126, 138
as control freak, 16, 38–39, 62
and conversion, 128
courage of, to persevere in
prayer and hope, ix
and dark night of the soul, 105
and dying to oneself, 33, 64
earthly support system for, vii
and Eli (son), vii, viii, ix,
15–19, 20, 21, 38–40,

44–45, 80, 105, 129–130,
138–139
and Ephraim (son), 16,
23–25, 27–28, 77
and EWTN, 15–16, 58, 140,
157
and Ezra (son), 68, 90, 157
faith of, to persevere in
prayer and hope, ix
as family man, 21
and Fr. Joe Breaux, 31, 33,
62, 64, 73
and Fr. Matthew "Padre"
Higginbotham, ix, x, 68,
68, 95–99
friendships of, 32
and God, viii, ix, x, 17, 21,
27–28, 32, 37–39, 44, 47,
49–50, 52, 60, 64, 81, 94,
105, 111, 116–117,
127–129, 137
on *The Gospel of Life*
(Catholic TV program), 157
grace, running on, 110
growing up, continuing, 21
happiness, more than having
right job, 29
hope, persevering in, ix
and human life, value of
from conception, 17
and Jesus Christ, 31–32,
40–41, 50, 52–53, 96, 124
and John Listi (friend), 61
and *Kairos* retreat, 62, 64
Lenten missions, leading, 157
letters to, 102, 110–111,
115–116, 118–121,
125–126, 137–140
and living in present
moment, 129
and the Lord, vii, 28, 41,

48–49, 61, 64
Man to Man conferences,
  addressing, 157
on manhood, ix, x, 31–34
and Mass, 37
and men's prayer group, vii,
  31–34
as minister, 126
and mother-in-law Ann, 81,
  88, 93, 108
on national TV, radio shows, 157
and Natural Family Planning
  (NFP), 21, 55–60, 79
obsessive-compulsive
  behavior of, 63
one-day-at-a-time approach
  to things, 129
parents of, vii, 44, 76, 108
photos of, *65, 66, 68–72,
  92–93, 157*
and physical fitness, 63
and praying, prayers, ix,
  17, 40–41, 45, 48, 80,
  88, 89, 93–94, 96–98 105,
  113–114, 124
presentations by, vii, 19, 34,
  70, 70, 81, 84, 95, 106,
  108, 117–118, 137, 157
as pro-life speaker. *See specific
  topics within this heading*
resolve of, to persevere in
  prayer and hope, ix
Respect Life gatherings,
  addressing, 157
retreats, leading, 62, 64, 157
and Rosary, 40–41, 113
and Sacrament of
  Reconciliation (confession), 64
Scripture, devouring, 48
on *Seize the Day* (Catholic
  TV program), 157

and self-confidence, 32
and self-discipline, 63
and self-discovery, 31
and self-examination, 62
and self-knowledge, 63
as speaker, vii, 19, 34–35,
  44, 51, 59, 62, 80–81,
  83–84, 90–91, 117, 123, 138
and special-needs child, ix,
  34–35, 37–38
spiritual advisors of, vii, ix,
  x, 68, 68, 95–99
spiritual maturity of, 32
on supporting family
  without steady paycheck, vii
as teacher, vii, ix, 16, 21, 23,
  28–29, 47–48, 81, 88,
  90–91, 93, 98–99, 101–102,
  110, 114, 123–124,
  126–128, 157
trapped in prison of own
  making, 73
travels of, telling Eli's story, 19
as writer, vi, vii, viii, 15–19,
  20, 47, 116, 123, 139, 157

Judice, Elijah Paul "Eli"
  adoring fans of, vii
  "army-crawling" of, vi, vii, 45
  as beautiful baby, 19
  birth of, vi, ix, 18, 43, 65
  brain surgery for, 103–104, 107
  catheterization of, 39, 48
  and Chiari malformation,
    103–104, 129
  and child-parent interactions,
    responses to, 129
  at Confirmation class, 138
  destined to be well known, vi
  doing better than doctors
    expected, 18

drum, banging on, 106, 108
earthly support system for, vii
emotional state of being, 129
and Ephraim (brother), 74, 75–77
and Ezra (brother), 81, 84
faith, his impact on, 118
and father, ix, 19, 21, 37–39, 157
First Communion, 67
in first grade, 21
and Fr. Manny Fernandez, 108–110
and Fr. Matthew "Padre" Higginbotham, 98
future of, 129–130
and gifts to the world, 129
given a chance at life, 19
and God, 18, 64, 137
growing up, continuing, 21
as happy baby, 19
and hydrocephalus, 43
"Immaculate Mary," playing, 129–130
impact of his life, 118
in utero, 38–39, 88, 108, 128
intelligence, at or above average, 18
in kindergarten, vii, 16, 21
left leg, surgical breaking and re-setting of, 102–103
living with as adventure, 18
and the Lord is with him, vii
love, eliciting from those around him, 129
medical needs, meeting, 80, 128
and miracles, Eli's life as, ix
and mother, vii, 19, 21, 39, 60, 157
music, bringing joy to, 128
music and, 106, 108, 128–129
naming of, 39
in Neonatal Intensive Care Unit, 43–44
occupational therapy for, 45
paralysis of, 73
photos of, *65–68, 70–72, 74, 82–83, 92–93, 106–107, 109*
physical dexterity, developing, 128
physical gains of, 105
physical impairments/ limitations, effect on, 64, 76
physical needs, meeting, 80, 128
physical therapy for, 21, 45, 102–103
piano, playing, 128–129
praying, prayer(s) for miracle for, 17
in Pre-K, 21
in second grade, vi, 21, 128
seizures, 21, 81, 94, 103–104
shunt in head, 43, 103, 108
smile of, 18, 106
as special-needs child, vi, viii, ix, 35, 37–38, 129
spina bifida, vi, viii, 15–18, 38–40, 43–44, 48, 65, 102–105, 106–107, 157
story of, vi–viii, 15–19, 20, 21, 26, 44, 139, 157
talking, very talkative, 18
at Tulane-Lakeside Hospital, Metairie, La., 43, 105–107, 107
and Vagus Nerve Stimulator implantation, 104
walking, 17–18, 76
wheelchair of, 16, 19, 63, 76, 103, 105–106
Judice, Ephraim
and Eli (brother), vii, ix, 74, 75–77
and father, 23–25, 27–28, 37, 157
and mother, 23–25, 27–28, 157

photos of, *68, 70, 72, 74, 92–93*
Judice, Ezra Matthew
  birth of, 94
  and father, 157
  and Fr. Matthew "Padre"
    Higginbotham, *68*, 98
  and mother, 157
  photos of, *68, 71, 72*

K*airos* ("On God's time"), 60,
  62, 64
kidney infections, 39
Kreeft, Peter, 115

L*earning* disabilities, *spina bifida*
  and, 17, 39
LeBlanc, Fr. Steve, 67
LeBlanc, Laynie, 137–139
Lent, 119
Lenten missions, 157
life, 17–19, 39
Listi, John, 61
Lord
  and agony in the garden, 40
  and Fr. Matthew P. "Padre"
    Higginbotham, 98
  grace of, 33
  is with Chad and Eli, vii
  and the Lord's love, 33
  and the Mysteries of the
    Rosary, 133–136
  seeking, serving, 61
  St. Ignatius, prayer by, 33
  standing naked before, 64
  trust in, growing in, 41
  uses things a man fears most, ix
  See also God
Lord's Prayer, 18
love, ix, x, 129–130, 133–136
  See also God; Jesus Christ; Lord
Luminous Mysteries, 40–41

M*ahner*, Ann and Karl, 117–121
Mahner, Miriam Grace, 118–121
Malone, Bishop Richard (Bishop
  of Buffalo), 70
Man to Man conferences, 157
manhood, vii, viii, ix, x, 31–34
map, of Eli's story in Louisiana, *26*
March for Life 2013, vii, *70, 92–93*
Mark 10:21-22, 50
Mary. *See* Blessed Virgin Mary
Mass, 33, 93
men, vii, ix, x, 18, 31–34
Metairie, La., vi, 43, 105, 107–108
miracles, ix
Mother Mary. *See* Blessed
  Virgin Mary
Mt. Carmel, Our Lady of. *See*
  Blessed Virgin Mary
Mysteries of the Rosary, 40–41,
  133–136

N*atural* Family Planning (NFP).
  See contraception
needs, four basic, 62–63
New York Post (newspaper),
  16–19, *20*, 157
NFP (Natural Family Planning).
  See contraception

O*'Brien*, Grace, 110–111
Old Testament, 125
O'Malley, Cardinal Sean
  (Archbishop of Boston), i, *69*
"on God's time" (*Kairos*), 62, 64
Our Father (prayer), 40, 108, 133
Our Lady of Mt. Carmel. *See*
  Blessed Virgin Mary

P*aralysis*, *spina bifida* and, 17
Parello, Christina, 137
Pellerin, Frank, 115–116
perseverance, grace of, 135

Pinto, Jim and Joy, 16, 140
Pope John Paul II, 58
Pope Paul VI, 57
praying, prayer(s)
    Apostles' Creed, 133
    to Blessed Virgin Mary, 40
    for Eli, 17–19, 37
    Eli's story, effect of on, vi
    by Fr. Manny Fernandez, 108
    by Fr. Matthew P. "Padre"
        Higginbotham, 96
    Glory Be's, 40
    to God, 27, 37, 39, 139
    God's mercy, praying for, 39
    Hail Holy Queen (prayer)
        (Reichenau), 97
    Hail Marys, 40, 108, 133
    to Holy Spirit, 108
    to Jesus Christ, 124
    to the Lord, prayer by St.
        Ignatius, 33
    Lord's Prayer, 18
    and men's prayer group, vii,
        31–34
    Our Fathers, 40, 108, 133
    to Our Lady of Mt. Carmel,
        88, *89*, 93–94
    persevering in, ix
    St. Ignatius, prayer by, 33
prisoner, praying for Eli, 18–19
pro-life
    books, vi–viii, 157
    conferences, 81, 84
    Mahner, Ann and Karl, as, 118
    message of Eli's story, 19
    movement, 137
    pro-life/pro-choice debate, 137
    rally, St. Matthew's Cathedral,
        Washington, D.C., 137
    speakers, 19, 44, 51, 59, 81,
        84, 117
Proverbs 27:17, 34

RCIA (Rite of Christian
    Initiation of Adults), 115
readings, spiritual, 58
Respect Life gatherings, 157
"Respect" (talk) (Judice), 34
retreats, 62, 64, 157
Richards, Fr Larry, i
River Jordan, 41
Robideaux, Brennan
    (screenwriter), 132
Romano, Mike, 140
Rosary, 40, *40*, 41, 45, 97,
    133–136
Russo, Fr. Michael, ii

Sacrament of Reconciliation
    (confession), 64
sacraments, as giving grace, 60, 64
Sacred Heart High School,
    Ville Platte, La., 83
sacrifice, x
sacrificial love, ix
sacrificial offering, NFP as, 60
salvation history, ix
Savior. *See* Jesus Christ
Scripture, 34, 48, 50, 130
Secular Franciscans (Third
    Order of St. Francis), 44
secular society, 31
self, dying to oneself, 33
selfless people, 32
shunt, in head, for *spina bifida*,
    43, 103, 108
Simon, Ray, 91, 93
Society of Jesus (Jesuits), 33
Soileau, Eric, 139–140
Sorrowful Mysteries, 40, 134
special-needs children
    challenges as, 129
    divorce rate for parents of, 48
    and DREAMS Foundation

of Acadiana (non-profit organization), 139
fear of having, ix, 37–38
and Peer Support class, 137–139
spina bifida
as birth defect, vi, 15–18, 105, 128, 157
and bowel control absence, 39
and catheterization, 39, 48
chance of occurring in other children of parents, 49
and Chiari malformation, 103–104, 129
effects on quality of life, 39
and hydrocephalus, 43
and kidney infections, 39
and learning disabilities, 17, 39
and paralysis, 17, 39
prenatal diagnosis, and abortion decision, 17, 39
prenatal diagnosis of, viii, 16, 38–40, 105, 108, 128
and shunt in head, 43, 103, 108
surgeries for, vi, 18, 21, 43–44, 65, 102–105, *106–107,* 108, 109, 129
spiritual advisors, vii
St. Ignatius, 33
St. Matthew's Cathedral, Washington, D.C., 137
St. Paul, 110, 126
St. Thomas More Catholic High School, Lafayette, La., 28–29, 32–34, 44–45, 48, 50–51, 56, 61–62, 64, 80–81, 90–91, 93, 98, 127, 157
men's prayer group at, 31–34
Staples, Tim, 115
STM. *See* St. Thomas More Catholic High School
suffering, 119, 121

Tears, and road to real manhood, x
The Gospel of Life (Catholic TV program), 157
The Lord. *See* Jesus Christ; Lord
The Lord's Prayer (prayer), 18
The Word Among Us (magazine), 157
The World Over (EWTN program), 16, 157
theological virtues, 130
Theology of the Body (lecture series) (Pope John Paul II), 48, 58
trials, and road to real manhood, x
Tulane-Lakeside Hospital, Metairie, La., 43, 105–106, *106–107*

University of Louisiana at Lafayette, 157
baseball team, *66*

Virgin Mary. See Blessed Virgin Mary
virtues, theological, 130

Waiting for Eli: A Father's Journey from Fear to Faith (Judice), vi, 19, 139, 157
"We plan, God laughs!" (refrigerator magnet), 47
White, Christopher, 124–127
Wichita, Kan., 81, 84
world, and manning-up, ix, x
worship, right worship, x

About the Author...

CHAD JUDICE is a nationally recognized motivational speaker, an award-winning author, and a teacher in the Theology Department at St. Thomas More Catholic High School in Lafayette, Louisiana.

He is the author of three inspiring pro-life, pro-faith books whose central character is his second son, who was born with *spina bifida.* The books are *WAITING FOR ELI: A Father's Journey from Fear to Faith; ELI'S REACH: On the Value of Human Life and the Power of Prayer;* and *GROWING WITH ELI: Our Journey into Life and Light.*

His articles have been published in the *New York Post* and *The Word Among Us.* He's been a guest on national TV and radio shows, including EWTN's *The World Over Live,* Catholic TV's *Seize the Day* and *The Gospel of Life.*

He is a Certified Catechist with certificates in Theology, Apologetics, Philosophy, and Church History from the New St. Thomas Institute, run by Dr. Taylor Marshall. He has given presentations to more than 100 audiences in 17 states, addressing Man to Man conferences and Respect Life gatherings and leading retreats as well as Lenten and Advent missions.

He earned a Bachelor of Science degree in Secondary Education Social Studies from the University of Louisiana at Lafayette in 2001. He is married to Ashley (*nee*) Guillotte, and they have three small children, Ephraim, Eli and Ezra. They make their home in Lafayette.

Inspiring Books
from
Acadian House Publishing

Growing With Eli
Our Journey into Life and Light

Growing With Eli is the third in an inspiring and heartwarming set of books that tell the story of a Lafayette, La., couple and their child, Eli, who was born with a birth defect called *spina bifida.* This volume, published when Eli was 9 years old, tracks the boy's growth from infancy to a healthy, happy youngster. At the same time, on a parallel track, the book chronicles Eli's father's growth in and understanding of his Catholic faith. (Author: Chad Judice. ISBN: 0-9995884-2-7. Price: $17.95, hardcover)

Eli's Reach
On the Value of Human Life and the Power of Prayer

Eli's Reach is the sequel to the inspiring heartwarming book, *Waiting for Eli,* which tells the story of a Lafayette, La., couple and their child, Eli, who was born with a birth defect called *spina bifida.* It is the story of how this child's life has touched the hearts and influenced the thinking of many. Hearing Eli's story has brought about a keener appreciation of the value of all human life and is credited with saving several unborn babies from abortion. (Author: Chad Judice. ISBN: 0-925417-25-4. Price: $14.95, softcover)

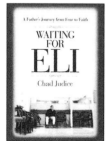

Waiting For Eli
A Father's Journey from Fear to Faith

A 176-page hardcover book about a Lafayette, La., couple and their infant son Eli who was born with a dreaded birth defect called *spina bifida.* It is an inspiring story of faith, hope and the power of prayer. The book takes us on an emotional roller coaster ride, starting with the day the author first learns of his son's medical condition. This moving story has a strong pro-life, pro-love message, and is made even more compelling by the author's descriptions of little miracles along the way.
(Author: Chad Judice. ISBN: 0-925417-65-3. Price: $16.95, hardcover)

Purses & Shoes For Sale
The Joys and Challenges of Caring for Elderly Parents

A 216-page book about the author's journey as a caregiver to her elderly parents in the twilight of their lives. Packed with suggestions on how to deal with issues encountered by adult children of the elderly. Includes a Q&A section with answers to frequently asked questions, plus a resources section with practical advice, useful websites and glossary of terms. (Author: Camille Pavy Claibourne. Harcover ISBN: 0-925417-96-3. Price: $17.95; Softcover ISBN: 0-925417-49-1. Price: $14.95)

Dying In God's Hands

A 152-page hardcover book that provides keen insights into the hearts and minds of the dying. It is based on a dozen or more interviews with terminally ill hospice patients, in which they share their hopes, dreams, fears and needs. The majority of the interviews provide evidence that faith in God and belief in the hereafter are the greatest strengths of the dying. Designed to comfort the dying and their loved ones, the book also contains a section of prayers and prose from all major world religions. (Author: Camille Pavy Claibourne. ISBN: 0-925417-64-5. Price: $16.95)

Freedom From Fear
A Way Through The Ways of Jesus The Christ

Everyone at one time or another feels fear, guilt, worry and shame. But when these emotions get out of control they can enslave a person, literally taking over his or her life. In this 142-page softcover book, the author suggests that the way out of this bondage is prayer, meditation and faith in God and His promise of salvation. The author points to the parables in the Gospels as Jesus' antidote to fears of various kinds, citing the parables of the prodigal son, the good Samaritan, and the widow and the judge. Exercises at the end of each chapter help make the book's lessons all the more real and useful. (Author: Francis Vanderwall. ISBN: 0-925417-34-3. Price: $14.95)

Getting Over the 4 Hurdles of Life

A 160-page hardcover book that shows us ways to get past the obstacles, or hurdles, that block our path to success, happiness and peace of mind. Four of the most common hurdles are "I can't / You can't," past failures or fear of failure, handicaps, and lack of self-knowledge. This inspiring book – by one of the top motivational speakers in the U.S. – is brought to life by intriguing stories of various people who overcame life's hurdles. Introduction by former LSU and NBA star Shaquille O'Neal. (Author: Coach Dale Brown. ISBN: 0-925417-72-6. Price: $17.95)

Infused
My Story of Cancer, Hope and Love

A 208-page hardcover autobiography of a young Austin, Texas, woman and her 5-year battle with breast cancer. The narrative takes us from her original diagnosis (only 3 months after she was married) through her search for the right doctor, chemotherapy, mastectomies, and the birth of her child by way of a surrogate. Written in a lively and very informative voice, the story is infused with hope, inspiration, and wit, with an extra dose of sarcasm. (Author: Courtney Bax Lasater, ISBN 0-925417-21-1. Price $22.95)

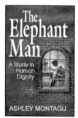

The Elephant Man
A Study in Human Dignity

The Elephant Man is a 138-page softcover book whose first edition inspired the movie and the Tony Award-winning play by the same name. This fascinating story, which has touched the hearts of readers throughout the world for over a century, is now complete with the publication of this, the Third Edition. Illustrated with photos and drawings of The Elephant Man. (Author: Ashley Montagu. ISBN: 0-925417-41-6. Price: $12.95.)

TO ORDER, list the books you wish to purchase along with the corresponding cost of each. For shipping, add $4 for the first book, and $1 per book thereafter. Louisiana residents add 9% tax to the cost of the books. Mail your order and check or credit card authorization (VISA/MC/AmEx) to: Acadian House Publishing, P.O. Box 52247, Lafayette, LA 70505. Or call (800) 850-8851. To order online, go to www.acadianhouse.com.